Hunter S. Thompson

Twayne's United States Authors Series

Frank Day, Editor

Clemson University

TUSAS 574

Hunter S. Thompson
Photogragh courtesy of Bob Krueger.

Hunter S. Thompson

William McKeen

University of Florida

Twayne Publishers
A Division of G. K. Hall & Co. • *Boston*

Hunter S. Thompson
William McKeen

Copyright 1991 by G. K. Hall & Co.
All rights reserved.
Published by Twayne Publishers
A division of G. K. Hall & Co.
70 Lincoln Street
Boston, Massachusetts 02111

Copyediting supervised by Barbara Sutton.
Book production by Janet Z. Reynolds.
Book design by Barbara Anderson.
Typeset by Compositors Corp., Cedar Rapids, Iowa.

First published 1991.
10 9 8 7 6 5 4 3 2 1

Library of Congress Cataloging-in-Publication Data

McKeen, William, 1954-
    Hunter S. Thompson / William McKeen.
        p.   cm. — (Twayne's United States authors series ; TUSAS 574)
    Includes bibliographical references (p.   ) and index.
    ISBN 0-8057-7624-9
    1. Thompson, Hunter S.   2. Journalists—United States—20th
century—Biography.   3. Thompson, Hunter S.—Literary art.
I. Title.   II. Series.
PN4874.T444M35   1991
070′.92—dc20
    [B]   90-45825

For my mother and father

Contents

Preface

When I was a reporter in the early 1970s, there were certain books that were passed around the newsroom of our small newspaper. We took turns reading them, then shared them with our colleagues, then discussed them over lunch and at our smoke-filled parties. A. J. Liebling's *The Press* was one of them, of course. *The Armies of the Night* was another. But the one we loved the most, the one we fought over because we wanted to read it again and again, was *Fear and Loathing in Las Vegas*.

It was my copy and I still have it. It is preserved in the file cabinet behind me, and in no condition to be handled. The spine of my paperback copy was quickly broken and pages had to be taped in. At one point, something or someone must have tried to eat it, because there are teeth marks all over the cover. (It would not surprise me if that was the work of one of my colleagues, in a gonzo frenzy.)

We all admired Hunter Thompson and, like fools, occasionally tried to write like him. So we had semigonzo accounts of common council meetings, press conferences, and speeches. They did not appear in the newspaper, being too weird and amateurish for our readers. But one of my colleagues, suffering from a severe case of gonzo envy, actually wrote a wonderful account of the visit to our small midwestern town by a failed vice-presidential candidate. Unfortunately, it was never published, though it was passed around and much admired. That reporter and I went to Naked City, Indiana, to cover the Mister and Miss Nude America contest. Our working title was "Fear and Loathing at Naked City" and we assumed the piece would appear in *Rolling Stone*. But although we labored a couple of long Saturdays on the project, we could not finish the article. It was too weird. We soon learned that we could not write like Hunter Thompson. Only one person could.

Several years later, I was teaching at a university in Kentucky, when Hunter Thompson was booked for an appearance. The day of his speech, the chairman of the speakers' board called and asked me to squire Thompson around and introduce him to the audience in the university auditorium. I said I would be pleased to do so, but began to worry as soon as I hung up the phone. As a reporter, I often worried when I was going to interview someone I had admired. I worried that such persons would disappoint me and I would never feel the same about their work.

But Thompson did not disappoint. We did not have much time together before the speech. He walked in and introduced himself, and shook hands like a normal human being. He was soft-spoken and polite, even if he did mumble a bit. He was certainly not the mad-dog reporter I had half-expected. We sat in a lounge near the stage and talked about my words of introduction and the format of the talk. It was a rather bluenose college, and so he would not be allowed his usual bottle of Wild Turkey on stage. Yet he needed *something* to keep his fires idling before facing the audience. He unzipped his athletic bag—his only luggage—parted the newspapers and clothes within, and pulled out a "live" Lowenbrau. It was open and foaming on his clothes. He quickly guzzled the last of the beer, then tossed the bottle across the room into the garbage can. "Let's go," he said.

In my introduction I referred to my time as a reporter and how Thompson was so much admired by journalists for being able to say the things that we could not say. I held up my battered and chewed copy of *Fear and Loathing in Las Vegas* and it disintegrated—pages flew out and lazily sailed to the auditorium floor. The audience laughed, but it helped me make a point. "This is an appreciated book," I said.

The talk was disappointing. Public speaking has never been Thompson's forte, and unless you were familiar with all of his works, his comments were difficult to follow. Many older faculty in attendance were at first bewildered and then disgusted. A large freak contingent had turned out and wanted to keep the conversation on drugs. Thompson was obliged to answer the questions that were asked, and the evening turned into a fiasco. People walked out. I asked a few questions, to steer the conversation back to writing and politics. But the audience wanted more amazing drug tales.

So it was a pleasure to write this book, to focus attention on Hunter Thompson's writing and not on his public persona or his status as a cartoon character in "Doonesbury." I do not believe Thompson is appreciated as a writer. His work seems disjointed, spontaneous, and loose, and it could only appear so if it were none of the above. It is the result of hard work and craftsmanship.

This book exists as an examination of Thompson's work, some of which is scattered and not readily available. Such is the nature of journalism. Most of chapter 2 is devoted to his early work. Chapter 3 discusses his experiences reporting and writing *Hell's Angels,* the book that put him on the map, as much for the stunt of riding with the Angels, as for any other reason. Chapter 4 concerns three critical articles in the evolution of Thompson's gonzo journalism, and chapter 5 is devoted to *Fear and Loathing in Las Vegas,* that style at fruition. His revolutionary coverage of presidential politics is the subject of chapter 6, and the last chapters are devoted to his relatively small output since the mid-1970s. It is unfortunate that Thompson chooses not to write as often as he did two decades ago.

I quote liberally from his works and apologize for summarizing passages of his writing. As New Journalism scholar Paul Thomas Meyers wrote, "A paraphrased Thompson certainly loses the feeling of that which he writes about and his position as a participant/observer." Indeed. Because of Thompson's strong stances, I use frequent and prolific passages from his work.

This book is also a rare biographical source on the man. Until now, the chief sources have been a couple of interviews and information in *Who's Who.* It is ironic that Thompson is usually the centerpiece of his work but really tells us very little about himself. I have attempted in chapter 1 to pull together as much information about him as seemed appropriate for a book essentially about his work.

Acknowledgments

I am pleased to thank several people who have helped with this project with actual labor, advice, and/or counsel.

Thomas Aubrey Beshear of the *Courier-Journal* in Louisville, Kentucky, helped with the research on Thompson's youth. Ruth Baxter aided me with locating other critical documents, and Juan Borras and Larry Strauss were able and enthusiastic research assistants. Danielle Berke tracked down some hard-to-find articles, and Wendi Sherman and Patricia DeMaras helped assemble the bibliography.

I am grateful for the support and encouragement of my colleagues at the University of Florida, particularly Jon Roosenraad, Jean Chance, Julie Dodd, John Griffith, and Rob Pierce. The research committee of the College of Journalism and Communications provided some support for this project, and I am indebted to Mary Ann Ferguson, that committee's chair.

The libraries at the University of Louisville and the University of Florida were invaluable hives for my research. I particularly want to acknowledge the wizardry of research librarian Dolores Jenkins at Florida.

Professor Murray Sperber of Indiana University was instrumental in introducing me to some of the nuances of Thompson's work, and I thank him for that. My former colleague Harry L. Allen was always incisive in his analyses of Thompson and other New Journalists.

Over the years, I have introduced many of my students to Thompson's writing, and they seemed to have been pleased that I did. Other students knew of his work and together we discovered and dissected each new article that was published. These long discussions often helped me deepen my appreciation for his writing. So I would like to thank Geoff Boucher, Bill Ward, Alan Judd, Greg Morelli, Lewis Gardner, Ed Bailey, and Clif Parker for a lot of good conversation.

Professor Frank Day of Clemson University, editor of the Twayne United States Authors Series, and Liz Traynor Fowler of Twayne Publishers were encouraging and worked hard to make this volume a worthy contribution to the series. I also thank Janet Z. Reynolds, Rob Winston and Barbara Sutton for their work editing the manuscript.

Hunter Thompson was cooperative. I am grateful for his time and for his writing. It has been a great pleasure to discover pieces I had never read before and to rediscover old favorites.

I would also like to thank my students, who have been supportive, encouraging, and understanding.

Chronology

1939   Hunter Stockton Thompson born 18 July to Jack and Virginia Thompson in Louisville, Kentucky.

1954   Jack Thompson dies.

1956   Enters U.S. Air Force.

1958   Leaves air force after his supervising officer discovers Thompson has been moonlighting for a civilian newspaper.

1959   Traveling in Caribbean, becomes correspondent for the *New York Herald Tribune*.

1961   Becomes South American correspondent for the *National Observer*.

1963   Returns to the United States. Marries Sandra Dawn, 19 May. Works as *Observer* correspondent and free-lance writer.

1964   Dispute with the *Observer*. Thompson tries writing a novel. Wife works as motel maid.

1965   "Motorcycle Gangs: Losers and Outsiders" published by the *Nation*. Thompson besieged with book contract offers.

1966   Rides with the Hell's Angels.

1967   *Hell's Angels* (subtitled "A Strange and Terrible Saga of the Outlaw Motorcycle Gang") published.

1968   Covers the presidential campaign. While in Chicago for August's Democratic National Convention, is beaten by the city's riot squad.

1969   Moves to Colorado, becomes involved in local politics, works on a novel.

1970   "The Kentucky Derby Is Decadent and Depraved" published by *Scanlan's*. Style is dubbed "gonzo." Runs for sheriff on the "Freak Power" ticket. Loses, but begins association with *Rolling Stone*.

1971   "Fear and Loathing in Las Vegas" serialized in *Rolling Stone*. Moves to Washington, D.C., to begin coverage of the presidential election campaign.

1972   *Fear and Loathing in Las Vegas* published in book form. Covers presidential campaign for *Rolling Stone*.

1973   *Fear and Loathing: On the Campaign Trail '72,* a collection of pieces on the campaign, published in book form. Sets up Washington, D.C., office for *Rolling Stone.*

1974   Covers Watergate and the Ali-Foreman fight in Zaire. Works on a novel to be called *Guts Ball.*

1975   Covers the fall of Saigon.

1977   Hits the college lecture circuit.

1979   *The Great Shark Hunt* published.

1981   Film based on Thompson's life, *Where the Buffalo Roam,* is released, starring Bill Murray as Thompson.

1983   *The Curse of Lono* published. Covers the sensational Roxanne Pulitzer divorce trial for *Rolling Stone.*

1984   Covers political conventions but does not publish anything about them. Supposedly at work on his novel *The Rum Diary.*

1985   Becomes columnist, working for the *San Francisco Examiner.* His account of the fall of Saigon, "Dance of the Doomed," is published ten years after the fact in *Rolling Stone.*

1988   *Generation of Swine* published.

1989   Becomes media critic for the *San Francisco Examiner.* Remains proprietor of the Woody Creek Rod and Gun Club in Woody Creek, Colorado.

1990   In trouble with the law for drugs and weapons charges. Publishes *Songs of the Doomed.* Working on *Polo is My Life.*

Chapter One
The Life and Times of Hunter S. Thompson

The crowd was getting restless. There were twelve hundred people in the nightclub, and they were angry because the featured attraction was overdue. It was Election Night 1988, and they had gathered to hear Hunter S. Thompson, the self-proclaimed "doctor of Gonzo journalism," deliver his commentary on the victory of George Bush. The Ritz dance hall in New York City had scheduled the iconoclastic journalist for an evening billed as "Fear and Loathing on Election Night." Thompson was supposed to take the stage at eight o'clock, but it was ten now, and the crowd was impatient.

Thompson's reputation as a college-campus lecturer had preceded him. He was known for arriving late, if at all, and for often mumbling incoherently. He never really lectured but instead answered questions from audiences. There were usually devoted fans in attendance who hung on his every word and queried him about the minutiae of his work. But most of the crowd would be annoyed that he was difficult to follow and spoke as if he expected everyone to have read everything he had published. It was like listening to one long in-joke. He would sit at a table on the stages of college auditoriums, holding forth with a bottle of Wild Turkey and a chunk of ice, making obscene comments greeted by titters from some members of the audience and by looks of disgust and outrage from others. Many would walk out. Thompson's reputation was large; he was a living legend to much of the crowd. This reputation made it difficult to travel or to work—particularly on such public work as journalism. As one observer wrote, "Thompson is a walking bundle of other people's expectations, unable to go anywhere or cover an event without people waiting for him to put on a show befitting a known maniac."[1]

Yet Thompson found these forays into the world of celebrity hard to turn down, if the price was right. For a few hours of talk, something he found painless to do, he could collect a significant amount of money. His talk was sometimes fascinating or maddening or perhaps both. So the idea of commentary on the election by Thompson seemed irresistible to the planners of the 1988 event. After all, he was still known for his unusual style of writing, which had briefly ignited new fires in political journalism in the early 1970s. His scorching characterizations of the powers-that-be had amused the press corps as much as a well-timed belch would have pleased a mischievous choirboy. And so the audience waited. They had paid twenty dollars at the door for the privilege of seeing Thompson and hearing his commentary.

Thompson finally took the stage at 10:30. He was difficult to understand because he slurred his words. After twenty minutes of rambling, he began taking questions from the audience. One angry man asked, "How can you justify charging $20, making us wait 2 ½ hours and then giving us this?" Thompson shrugged. "I do this all the time," he said. One participant was quoted in the next day's *New York Post:* "They wanted some political insight. What they got was a drunk old man." The *Post* called the evening a "full-fledged fiasco." Despite the heckling, Thompson did not get upset with the audience. He merely showed off a hunting rifle, which inspired some members of the audience to leave.[2]

It was a sad and discouraging spectacle in the life of America's premier outlaw journalist. Thompson's career has had the trajectory of a shooting star, at its brilliant best in the early 1970s, when he found in Richard Nixon the muse his political satire needed. As Nixon's star fell, so, in some ways, did Thompson's. His output slowed considerably after 1974 and he seemed to coast on his image and reputation. His major book of the late 1970s was *The Great Shark Hunt,* a collection of previously published pieces—some of them fifteen years old. He was the subject of the cult film *Where the Buffalo Roam,* in which actor Bill Murray did a brilliant imitation of Thompson. He became the model for Uncle Duke, a regular character in Garry Trudeau's "Doonesbury."

Thompson remained a news maker and a pop-culture icon, despite his slowed output. Stories would hit the press of another Thompson campus appearance or another canceled date or another near miss with the law. To many, it was a sad residue, the fall of a brilliant but troubled man. But was his work—admittedly not as profound as it had been in his glory years—more mature and perhaps better than the fiery works of old? And was he perhaps just tired of his fame and living up to an image that was impossible—and unhealthy—to maintain?

Early Life

Hunter Stockton Thompson weighed eleven pounds at birth. He was born in Louisville, Kentucky, on 18 July 1939. His father was Jack

Thompson, an insurance salesman who died when his eldest son was fifteen. His mother, Virginia, had to raise her three sons alone and saw Hunter through a troubled adolescence. Thompson had often been difficult as a child but he learned relatively early how to manipulate people, to charm them and get his way. He passed through public schools in Louisville without much effort and was active in the Presbyterian church, as was his mother's wish. He even represented his church at a youth convention in North Carolina when he was in junior high school.

Thompson first made the news when he was only fourteen. He had taken a job at the First National Bank of Louisville in 1953, to help out his mother after his father's death. On his first payday, he was paid with a fifty-dollar bill. At lunchtime, he used part of his break to walk to another bank downtown, where he intended to add the fifty dollars to a savings account. He made out the deposit slip, then searched frantically through his pockets for the money. It was gone. "I didn't have it long enough to realize it was really mine," he told a reporter.[3] The short feature on Thompson's loss that appeared in the *Courier-Journal* attracted the attention of Alonzo Robinson, an employee at the Bridle Bit, the restaurant where Thompson had eaten lunch before going to the bank. Robinson had found the money and returned it to Thompson, who was so grateful that he gave the cook a reward.[4]

Despite the responsibility of having a job and helping out at home, Thompson "grew into juvenile delinquency," as he put it. Although he was popular and a regular at parties in "good homes," when he learned to drive, his life changed dramatically. He would often end up cruising the streets of Louisville for hours as his mother, recently widowed, waited at home alone, praying her son would come safely back to her. He would have a couple of beers, meet some friends, and maybe take a dare. Sometimes he would get into a fight.

Some began to dismiss Thompson as a hoodlum, a good boy gone bad, another example of what ill could befall a fatherless boy. "He was the neighborhood terror," one parent remembered. "Some of my friends wouldn't let their daughters go out with him."[5] But to others Thompson had a great deal of charm. Classmates lined up on the sidewalk outside his house just for the privilege of walking to school with him, of being seen with him, of enjoying his company. He had a rough-edged charm that was attractive to his friends. He was obviously intelligent—what other juvenile delinquent carried around Plato's *Republic?*—and could be friendly, polite, and intensely loyal to friends.

"Hunter always had this peculiar quality," Virginia Thompson said. "[It was] a kind of charisma. It's like being in the eye of a tornado, being in a room with him. You never know what's going to happen next. And yet he doesn't seem to be doing anything. There's just this terrible sense of expectation and excitement when Hunter's around. He's always had this fascination for people, ever since he was a little boy."[6]

When Thompson was seventeen, he and two other boys were arrested and charged with a robbery of a service-station attendant. The service-station attendant, his date, and another couple were parked near a fountain in a park, talking, when Thompson and his friends drove up behind them and parked. Apparently, two of the boys approached the two couples and first asked for a cigarette. When the service-station attendant offered one, one of the three boys grabbed his arm and held it, threatening to pull a gun. They took all the money the service-station attendant had in his wallet, which amounted to eight dollars. The three boys drove away, but the attendant got their license number and they were soon tracked down by police.[7]

One of Thompson's friends was not identified by name in one of the newspapers. Ralston Steenrod was referred to only as "a high-school football star with no previous record" by the *Louisville Times,* although the *Courier-Journal* identified him. Thompson's other companion, Samuel Stallings, had been arrested once before. Thompson, the *Louisville Times* noted, had been arrested three times previously. The article in that day's newspaper reported that the three boys admitted robbing the attendant but offered no motive. "We were just driving around," one of them told police.[8]

The sentencing came a month later. Steenrod was placed on probation, and Stallings was fined fifty dollars on an amended charge of disorderly conduct and placed under a five-hundred-dollar peace bond for six months.

But Thompson was not so lucky. The juvenile court judge was not as lenient with Thompson because of his record—previous arrests for underage drinking and vandalism. Virginia Thompson appeared in court and made an emotional appeal in her son's behalf. "Please don't send him to jail," Mrs. Thompson begged. "What do you want me to do?" the judge asked. "Give him a medal?" Further pleas were made for Thompson by the father of his companions that night and the attorney retained to represent the three of them. The attorney argued that Thompson should be released and allowed to enlist in the air force, "which would make a man out of him." The judge was not moved by the plea. While Thompson stood before him in tears, the judge sentenced the teenager to sixty days in jail. As he did so, a girl in the courtroom leaped to her feet and yelled, "But he tried to help us!" The girl had been in the victim's car the night of the robbery and said that it was Stallings who had threatened them and that Thompson tried to calm him down. Yet the judge said he had to consider the young man's record in making his decision.[9] The two couples tried to intercede for Thompson, but the judge would not hear their pleas. "I feel I've done you an injustice by waiting so long to take a positive step," the judge told Thompson.[10]

The incident kept Thompson and Stallings from graduating with the rest of their class at Male High School and they were placed on indefinite suspension. Steenrod was allowed to go through commencement. The principal said he took the action "on the basis of their cumulative records."[11]

Thompson turned eighteen in jail and at the end of thirty days was released early and lectured by the judge. "You are not on probation," he said. "But you will be watched." An article on Thompson's release noted that court officials thought he was making progress on "mending his ways."[12]

Youthful Magnetism

In the period after the incident in the park, Thompson became friends with the two couples he had supposedly robbed. That fact says something of the magnetism Virginia Thompson claims her son had even then. Thompson carried his magnetism with him into adulthood and his celebrated career. Actor Bill Murray, who got to know Thompson well during the making of *Where the Buffalo Roam,* echoed Mrs. Thompson: "With Hunter, you absolutely never forget that he's around. You constantly have to deal with him. I mean, that is the thing. Being around him, you get a lot. He's a wonderful friend and a joy to know. But somehow, you have to pay for it."[13]

Thompson had two younger brothers, Davison and James. Kate Stout, a friend of James's, recalled the first time she saw Hunter Thompson, when she was fifteen:

[W]e were sitting on the porch swing, awaiting his great arrival. Of course, his legend preceded him. He'd been a freelance journalist in South America but most recently had survived almost being murdered while researching the Hell's Angels. Jim adored him and sang his praises. Even so, I was not in the least prepared for the effect he had. Loose, lanky, walking up the path just like anybody's big brother— only different, critically different. I knew he was weird, I knew he was tough, and I knew he used language I wasn't even allowed to acknowledge when it was spray-painted on the walls of underpasses. But he wasn't a thug. He wasn't a greaser from the 50s or a hippie from the 60s. He could have been almost anybody else, casually dressed. Except for the aura. A presence. He strolled in the house as if he'd only been gone for a matter of hours, instead of months, the two of us trailing after. Time and the world seemed to stand still. Something else had taken over. It was a kind of energy, a power to unwittingly captivate.[14]

The Thompson that Stout met was finally making his name as a big-name journalist, after getting off to a rather rough start in the business. At eighteen, he escaped Louisville, into the U.S. Air Force, at the urging of the officers of the court. In the air force, he lied about his background to become editor of the Eglin Air Force Base newsletter, at the huge post in the Florida panhandle. His superiors recognized his talent. "Airman Thompson possesses outstanding talent in writing," the chief of the base's information services wing wrote. "He has imagination, good use of English, and can express his thoughts in a manner that makes interesting reading." But Thompson infuriated the officers with his surly attitude and his twisted sense of humor. "Airman Thompson has consistently written controversial material and leans so strongly to critical editorializing that it was necessary to require that all his writing be thoroughly edited before release," his personnel report stated.[15]

When Thompson began moonlighting for a local civilian publication, he was suspended for his display of "poor judgement." His superior lamented that Thompson, "although talented, will not be guided by policy or personnel advice and guidance. Sometimes his rebel [sic] and superior attitude seems to rub off on other airmen staff members. He has little consideration for military bearing or dress and seems to dislike the service and wants out as soon as possible. Consequently, it is requested that Airman Thompson be assigned to other duties immediately. . . ." Reportedly, Thompson was threatened with reassignment to Iceland when it was revealed that he had been writing for the civilian paper under a pseudonym—Sebastian Owl. Despite the reports from his superiors, Thompson managed to secure an honorable discharge in 1958, two years before his enlistment was up.

After his discharge, Thompson got fired from his first job, with the *Record* in Middletown, New York. He worked at a number of other publications and was fired from many of them. Once, he destroyed his editor's car. At another paper, he insulted an advertiser and demolished a candy machine in the break room. He was dismissed from his job as a trainee at *Time* magazine for his poor attitude toward work. (During his stint with the Luce empire, Thompson had spent a lot of time at his desk, typing Fitzgerald and Faulkner verbatim to try to understand the pace of their writing.)[16] He managed to outlast a bowling magazine he worked for in Puerto Rico, and after it folded he vowed to give up journalism.

Under the influence of the beat poets and Jack Kerouac's *On the Road,* Thompson became a drifter, working his way cross-country to California. He ended up on the rugged Big Sur peninsula, laboring on the great American novel. It was never published.[17] He became one of the beatniks of San Francisco's North Beach area and found other midwestern renegades.

Thompson then moved to South America, and from that far-flung location he made his first splash in America as a journalist. He began stringing for the *National Observer,* Dow Jones's much-admired weekly that exploited the thoughtful news feature style pioneered by its sister publication, the *Wall Street Journal.* The *Journal*'s left-hand column on the front page of every edition featured an expertly crafted article devoted to a social issue, seen through the eyes of a character exemplifying a pressing human problem. The *Observer* was full of such features, complemented by reviews and surveys of the arts. It competed with *Time* and *Newsweek* more than any other newsprint publication, and it lasted a little over a decade.

The *Observer* wanted color, and it wanted dispatches from all around the world. Thompson became a regular contributor, often landing his pieces on the front page, where they would get elegant display. He wrote about excitement and romance in some of the still-wild parts of South America, sketching the lives of tin miners, jungle bandits, and smugglers.[18] For the first time, Thompson was making good money and having a good time. But even the "good times" got old: "Rio was the end of the foreign correspondent's tour. I found myself 25 years old, wearing a white suit, and rolling dice at the Domino Club—the foreign correspondent's club. And here I thought, 'Jesus Christ, what am I gonna do now?' Then, I would roll dice more and write less and worry about it until I'd have a nervous breakdown. It makes you change whatever you're doing. So I just came back here, in sort of a frenzy of patriotism—Kennedy, Peace Corps."[19]

Thompson returned to the United States, married Sandra Dawn on 19 May 1963, and resumed his Bay Area existence, serving as the *Observer*'s roving North American correspondent. He did a number of features on American outcasts and radicals and eventually provoked some friction with the *Observer*'s editors. Thompson resigned after a disagreement over coverage of the free speech movement at the University of California at Berkeley. The *Observer*'s editors did not accept Thompson's contention that the Berkeley protests were the beginning of bigger things.[20] "I decided, 'Fuck journalism,' " Thompson said, "and I went back to writing novels."[21]

But the novel writing did not go well. His wife worked as a motel maid to keep the money coming in while Thompson struggled with his writing.

He drove a cab and did odd jobs. "I tried every kind of thing," he remembered. "I used to go down at five o'clock every morning and line up with the winos on Mission Street, looking for work handing out grocery-store circulars and shit like that. I was the youngest and healthiest person down there, but nobody would ever select me. I tried to get weird and rotten-looking; you know, an old Army field jacket, scraggly beard, tried to look like a bad wino. But even then, I never got picked out of the line-up."[22] He was living from paycheck to paycheck, and the checks were not regular. He wrote a piece about the Berkeley radicals that impressed the editors of the *Nation,* which purchased it. When Carey McWilliams, editor of the *Nation,* wrote Thompson in 1965 and asked him to do a piece on the Hell's Angels motorcycle gang, Thompson leapt at the opportunity.

The World of the Angels

Getting into the world of the Hell's Angels was difficult for an outsider, even someone like Hunter Thompson. Even though Thompson approached the motorcycle gang in a madras coat and wing tips, he felt that the Angels could tell he was "a little strange," perhaps because he was paying serious attention to them. As he remembered, "I just went out there and said, 'Look, you guys don't know me, I don't know you, I heard some bad things about you, are they true?' " The Angels were happy to talk. "Until then," Thompson said, "all the Hell's Angels stories had come from the cops. They seemed a little stunned at the idea that some straight-looking writer for a New York literary magazine would actually track them down to some obscure transmission shop in the industrial slums of south San Francisco. They were a bit off-balance at first, but after 50 or 60 beers, we found a common ground, as it were."[23]

Editor McWilliams liked the article and suggested that Thompson develop it into a book. After the *Nation* published the piece, book contracts came pouring in. One publisher was willing to give Thompson fifteen hundred dollars merely for signing a statement of intent. As Thompson recalled his excitement over all the attention: "Christ! For $1,500, I'd have done the definitive text on hammerhead sharks and stayed with them in the water for three months."[24] Thompson quickly signed a contract with Random House. He spent six months writing the first half of the book and wrote the last half in a frantic four-day period. "I got terrified about the deadline," Thompson remembered. "I actually thought they were going to cancel the contract if I didn't finish the book exactly on time. I was in despair over the thing, so I took the electric typewriter and about four quarts of Wild Turkey and just drove north on 101 until I found a motel that looked peaceful, checked in and stayed there for four days. Didn't sleep, ate a lot of speed, went out every morning and got a hamburger at McDonald's and just wrote straight through for four days—and that turned out to be the best part of the book."[25] His eventual beating at the hands of the gang provided the perfect coda for the resulting *Hell's Angels,* subtitled "A Strange and Terrible Saga of the Outlaw Motorcycle Gang" (1967). During his work on that book, Thompson used LSD for the first time and began a long infatuation with drugs that eventually permeated his writing. Novelist Ken Kesey, who had written *One Flew over the Cuckoo's Nest* and *Sometimes a Great Notion,* was the first to give the hallucinogenic to Thompson. "Ken Kesey wanted to meet some of the Angels," Thompson recalled, "so I introduced him and he invited them all down to his place in La Honda. It was a horrible, momentous meeting and I thought I'd better be there to see what happened when all this incredible chemistry came together. And, sure as shit, the Angels rolled in—about 40 or 50 bikes—and Kesey and the other people were offering them acid. And I thought, 'Great creeping Jesus, what's going to happen now?' " Thompson thought Kesey and his companions did not realize the violence of which the Angels were capable, and Thompson feared what they might do under the influence of the drug: "I was sure it was going to be a terrible blood, rape and pillage scene, that the Angels would tear the place apart. And I stood there, thinking, 'Jesus, I'm responsible for this. I'm the one who did it.' I watched those lunatics gobbling the acid and I thought, 'Shit, if it's gonna get this heavy I want to be as fucked up as possible.' "[26]

Thompson ingested 800 milligrams of LSD, which he said nearly blew his head off. His head would never be the same, as drugs became a major part of his life-style. Fortunately, the LSD had a calming effect on the Angels and there was no violence.

After the success of *Hell's Angels,* Thompson continued writing for magazines and again considered a novel. He flirted with political reporting and even had a rare hour-long interview with Richard Nixon during the New Hampshire primary in 1968. The ground rule for the interview was that Thompson not ask Nixon any political questions. So they discussed pro football, a subject on which Nixon and Thompson were expert. Thompson nearly killed Nixon, himself, and those standing around them at an airport when he leaned over the gas tank of Nixon's private plane with a lighted cigarette.[27] Of Nixon, Thompson said, "He seemed like a Republican echo of Hubert Humphrey. Just another sad old geek limping back into politics for another beating. It never occurred to me that he would ever be president. Johnson hadn't quit at that point, but I sort of sensed he was going to and I figured Bobby Kennedy would run—so that even if Nixon got the Republican nomination, he'd just take another stomping by another Kennedy. So I thought it would be nice to go to New Hampshire, spend a couple of weeks following Nixon around and then write his political obituary."[28] Thompson stayed on the campaign trail most of 1968, writing articles for *Pageant,* until the police riot at the Democratic National Convention in Chicago. Thompson said he was "really jerked around" politically after witnessing the scene on the streets of Chicago. He saw "innocent people beaten senseless" and was himself smashed with a billy club.[29] "I went to the Democratic convention as a journalist and returned as a raving beast," he said.[30]

Thompson moved to Aspen, Colorado, and became involved with a group of friends dissatisfied with the burgeoning developments around the mountain community. As he said to one of his friends, "[W]e *have* to get into politics—if only in self-defense."[31] Thompson became a major mover and shaker in Aspen's "Freak Power" campaign to radicalize the Rockies. With an attorney friend named Joe Edwards, Thompson decided to enter politics. Edwards ran for mayor on an antidevelopment stance and was defeated. Thompson ran for sheriff in a later election, espousing much the same line. "It got a little heavy," Thompson remembered. "I announced that the new sheriff's posse would start tearing up the streets the day after the election—every street in Aspen, rip 'em up with jackhammers and replace the asphalt with sod. I said we were going to use the sheriff's office mainly to harass real-estate developers."[32] The campaign platform also called for renaming Aspen "Fat City" and punishing dealers of bad drugs with humiliation in public stocks. Thompson decided to seek national publicity for his campaign, and so he took a trip to San Francisco.

Jann Wenner was the twenty-three-year-old "boy editor" of *Rolling Stone.* The magazine, started in the offices of an old brewery in 1967, had already made a name for itself nationally by publishing the nude cover photograph of John Lennon and Yoko Ono from their controversial album *Two Virgins.* The magazine was devoted mostly to rock and roll, but Wenner was privately considering branching into other areas to broaden its appeal. One of his assistant editors had warned him that the man who had come to see him was "out of the ordinary." But Wenner was not prepared for Hunter Thompson.

Thompson was wearing a gray woman's wig, chino shorts, a wild Mexican shirt, and his now-trademark aviator sunglasses. He carried a six-pack of beer, which he drank during the course of his meeting with Wenner.

When Thompson got up to go to the bathroom, Wenner turned to one of his associates and said, "I know I'm supposed to be the spokesman for the counterculture and all that, but what the fuck is *this?*"[33] Despite Wenner's initial concern about Thompson's appearance, he and Thompson forged an intense personal and professional relationship that proved—professionally, at least—to be mutually beneficial. "Freak Power in the Rockies" was published in *Rolling Stone* on 1 October 1970, thus beginning Thompson's colorful association with the magazine. A follow-up story detailed his narrow loss of the election.

Until he went to work for *Rolling Stone,* Thompson's best association had been with *Scanlan's,* a short-lived weekly magazine started by Warren Hinckle after his *Ramparts* magazine had failed. Hinckle was one of the few editors willing to take a chance on Thompson. Drinking with friends in Aspen one night early in 1970, Thompson had begun to reminisce about Louisville and the Kentucky Derby. He decided this spectacle needed to be truthfully chronicled and that he was the reporter for the job. He called San Francisco, woke up Hinckle, and nearly demanded the assignment. Hinckle agreed and dispatched English illustrator Ralph Steadman to Kentucky to meet Thompson.[34] How they got the story became the subject of the story. Process became art. Owing to the intense pressure of the *Scanlan's* deadline, Thompson was breaking. "I'd blown my mind, couldn't work," Thompson said. "So finally I just started jerking pages out of my notebook and numbering them and sending them to the printer. I was sure it was the last article I would ever do for anybody. Then when it came out, there were massive numbers of letters, phone calls, congratulations, people calling it a 'great breakthrough in journalism.' And I thought . . . if I can write like this and get away with it, why should I keep trying to write like the *New York Times?* It was like falling down an elevator shaft and landing in a pool of mermaids."[35] Bill Cardoso, a writer Thompson had met while covering the Nixon campaign, sent Thompson an admiring note, calling the article "pure Gonzo."[36] And so Hunter Thompson finally had a name for what he did: gonzo journalism.

Wenner published another extended piece by Thompson in April 1971. "Strange Rumblings in Aztlan" told the story of murdered *Los Angeles Times* columnist Ruben Salazar and the effect his death had on the Hispanic community of East Los Angeles. It was another example of Thompson's first-person journalism, in which getting the story became the story. Researching the piece also led Thompson to Oscar Zeta Acosta, a Hispanic attorney with whom he would become close friends.

Failure Turns into *Fear and Loathing*

Thompson turned two aborted magazine assignments into his next *Rolling Stone* piece (actually, a two-part work) that was published as a book the next year. *Sports Illustrated* wanted Thompson to cover the Mint 400 motorcycle race in the desert. He took off for Las Vegas with Acosta and had a number of adventures, none of them having to do with motorcycle racing. Thompson was ready to return to Los Angeles when Wenner reached him with an assignment to cover the National District Attorneys Conference on Drug Abuse, also meeting in Las Vegas. Again, the reason for his being in the city was largely ignored and the process of getting (or not getting) the story became the story.

It also became his masterpiece. *Fear and Loathing in Las Vegas* (1972) was Thompson's breakthrough. The two protagonists—Raoul Duke (Thompson) and Dr. Gonzo (Acosta)—run amok on the Las Vegas strip, consuming enormous quantities of drugs and terrorizing everyone in sight. Immediately there were questions. Was this *journalism?* Was this all true? Could anyone ingest everything Thompson claims they ingested and live to tell? The author merely said, "I lost all track of the ratio of what was true and what was not."[37] Librarians were also confused. *Fear and Loathing in Las Vegas* has been classified as journalism, a novel, and a travelogue. Reaction to the book was strong and largely positive. The *New York Times Book Review* noted: "The form that reached apotheosis in [Norman Mailer's] *The Armies of the Night* reaches the end of its rope in *Fear and Loathing,* a chronicle of addiction and dismemberment so vicious that it requires a lot of resilience to sense that the author's purpose is more moralizing than sadistic. He is moving in a country where only a few cranky saviors—Jonathan Swift, for one—have gone before. And he moves with the cool integrity of an artist indifferent to his reception."[38]

The serialized version of *Fear and Loathing* had just been published when Thompson convinced Wenner—over the objections of most of the *Rolling Stone* staff—that the magazine should cover the 1972 presidential election campaign full tilt. He volunteered his services, and Wenner agreed.

With his wife and young son, Juan, Thompson set up base camp in Washington, D.C., enduring what he called a "year of grim exile." At the beginning of the campaign, Thompson was shut out from many of the activities that the major heavyweights of the American press were allowed to cover. That was fine with him. Exclusion from the establishment was nothing new to Thompson, and he preferred working apart from the crowd. Many of the other reporters had no idea who he was and had never heard of

Rolling Stone. Soon, however, the reporters began reading Thompson's colorful articles and came to admire him. He wrote the things they could only think and talk about; they could never publish what Thompson was publishing in *Rolling Stone.* Thompson became a hero of sorts to some of the straight reporters, but he did not easily forgive them for the cold shoulder he had received in the early days of the campaign trail. He urged his Wenner-appointed assistant, Timothy Crouse, to study the press corps carefully. "Watch those swine day and night," he advised. "Every time they fuck someone who isn't their wife, every time they pick their nose, every time they have their hand up their ass, you write it down. Get all of it. Then we'll lay it all on them in October."[39] Crouse had been assigned to keep Thompson in control and on deadline. Thompson encouraged Crouse, though, to work on longer articles and presented his case to Wenner. He worked to get Crouse better, more prestigious assignments. From his work with Thompson, Crouse produced a modern masterpiece of political journalism, *The Boys on the Bus* (1973).

Thompson observed no sacred cows in his reporting of the campaign. Edmund Muskie, the leading Democratic candidate, betrayed the desperation of a "farmer with terminal cancer trying to get a loan on next year's crop." Hubert Humphrey "campaigned like a rat in heat." Thompson admired George McGovern, the eventual Democratic nominee, but had no kind words for his former football buddy, Richard Nixon. At the end of the campaign he wrote:

This may be the year when we finally come face to face with ourselves; finally just lay back and say it—that we really are just a nation of 220 million used car salesmen with all the money we need to buy guns, and no qualms at all about killing anybody else in the world who tries to make us uncomfortable.

. . . [W]hat a fantastic monument to all the best instincts of the human race this country might have been, if we could have kept it out of the hands of greedy little hustlers like Richard Nixon. . . .

Jesus! Where will it end? How low do you have to stoop in this country to be president?[40]

Politics had been a success for Thompson and for *Rolling Stone.* Wenner asked Thompson to establish a "National Affairs Desk" in Washington. This endeavour proved to be time-consuming for Thompson, who did not appreciate such donkeywork on the heels of a year of campaign coverage and a nightmarish several weeks turning his dispatches from the road into a book, *Fear and Loathing: On the Campaign Trail '72* (1973). Thompson managed to set up a bureau, but it fell to Timothy Crouse and eventually Richard Goodwin, a former speech writer for Presidents Kennedy and Johnson, to keep it going.

Thompson was amused by Watergate and provided the magazine with several good pieces chronicling the unraveling of the Nixon administration. But his output slowed considerably, and some assignments bore no fruit. While in Zaire in 1974 to cover the Muhammad Ali–George Foreman fight, Thompson contracted malaria and did not file a story. He was sent to Saigon to cover its fall in 1975, but the article he wrote did not appear in *Rolling Stone* until more than a decade later. His last major splash in the 1970s came with a *Rolling Stone* article devoted to Jimmy Carter. "Jimmy Carter and the Great Leap of Faith" was Thompson's account of meeting Carter and hearing his address to law school graduates at the University of Georgia. The speech was reprinted in the magazine, and the cover line Wenner selected for that issue read, "An Endorsement, with Fear and Loathing." Thompson was not pleased.

Yet he stayed with the magazine, returning to Las Vegas to finally produce an acceptable article about Muhammad Ali ("Last Tango in Vegas"). For *Rolling Stone*'s tenth-anniversary issue in 1977, Thompson wrote about Oscar Zeta Acosta, who had disappeared. Thompson's intention with "The Banshee Screams for Buffalo Meat" (Acosta was known as "The Brown Buffalo") was to libel Acosta so that he would reappear to refute the charges. When he did not, Thompson assumed he was dead—perhaps murdered.

Thompson chose to close the decade with a retrospective of his work, *The Great Shark Hunt* (1979). This varied, jumbled, disorganized collection was a huge best-seller. It included a mock press release he had written while stationed at Eglin Air Force Base, several selections from the *National Observer,* and the early pieces for the *Nation* and the *New York Times,* as well as articles for *Playboy* and most of his major pieces for *Rolling Stone.*

After the publication of that book, Thompson was relatively quiet as a writer. He had become a popular college lecturer in the late 1970s and had achieved a healthy income. His appearances were notable for the number of questions he was asked about drug use. He answered them faithfully, and often his campus appearances were not at all about writing or politics but instead were collections of "amazing drug tales." Perhaps he felt some shame or embarrassment about this aspect of his public persona. He agreed once to speak at the University of Kentucky on the condition that neither his mother nor his brothers be in the audience. Both parties would no doubt be uncomfortable with the public Hunter Thompson on display. "I am fiercely proud of Hunter because he's made it on his own, with help from no one," Virginia Thompson said. "But I strongly disapprove of his lifestyle. We [the family] all think he's killing himself with drugs."[41]

He largely rested on his laurels and watched his legend made into a film called *Where the Buffalo Roam*. Loosely based on his relationship with Acosta, the film fictionalized a good deal—changing names and places. It was a poor movie but contained a brilliant performance: Bill Murray's impersonation of Hunter Thompson. Thompson was a consultant and co-scriptwriter and provided the voice-over narration.

His output dropped off dramatically for much of the 1980s. He covered the sensational Roxanne Pulitzer divorce trial for *Rolling Stone* in 1983 and that fall published a book about deep-sea fishing off the coast of Hawaii, *The Curse of Lono* (1983).

His divorce intervened. After seventeen years of a stormy marriage, Hunter and Sandy Thompson were divorced in 1980, with Sandy getting custody of their son, Juan. Friends described the break as neither bitter nor sudden, and perhaps a good thing for their long-term relationship. "Sandy probably had some hellish years with him," Virginia Thompson said of her son's marriage. "Hunter is extremely difficult to live with. He was difficult to live with as a child. But she still adores him—says she'll never love anyone else but Hunter. And I think Hunter—as much as Hunter can—still loves her."[42] Sandy Thompson moved to Aspen and lives less than a half-hour's drive from her ex-husband's home in Woody Creek.

In the early 1980s, Thompson again worked on a novel and again it was not published. In 1985, he surprised the journalistic world by taking a position as a columnist for the *San Francisco Examiner.* He could not write for a daily newspaper in quite the same way he had written for *Rolling Stone,* and so his columns were fairly free of the drug references and obscenities of his earlier work. As a result, many critics suggested that Gonzo Journalist No. 1 was tamed. He published his columns as *Generation of Swine* (1988), with the subtitle "Gonzo Papers, volume 2" (*The Great Shark Hunt* was volume 1). In the introduction, Thompson wrote, "I have spent half my life trying to get away from journalism, but I am still mired in it—a low trade and a habit worse than heroin, a strange seedy world of misfits and failures."[43]

In spite of his efforts to break away from journalism by writing novels, Thompson has found his success with nonfiction. To him, it has become an addiction of sorts. If he is unable or unwilling to publish his fiction, it could be because he realizes it might not stand up to the power of his journalism.

Thompson remains an important figure on the American landscape, despite his slowed output of the past decade. New generations of college students discover his work and turn out to hear his "lectures." And people will apparently pay twenty dollars to sit in a night club audience and hear him talk about politics.

Thompson, by his own description, is lazy: "[W]riting is a hard dollar. I am a lazy bastard. I am a hillbilly. I don't see much sense in working hard all your life if you can't rest for a minute. This mania of having to work hard all the time—I would much rather be on my boat. I would like to be a fisherman. I would like to con these people into letting me take them fishing. 'Gonzo Tours.' I have been missing something all this time; I could have been [in Key West] running a fifty-foot yacht doing nothing at all."[44]

Despite his self-proclaimed sloth, Thompson's work stands as a vital chronicle of a turbulent time in American history. In the end, his may be the truest telling of the story of the 1960s and 1970s.

Chapter Two
The Reporter

One of the most surprising things about Hunter S. Thompson's work is its consistency. It is not something one would expect from a writer known mostly for inconsistency. It is also surprising, considering that Thompson's wildest prose seems to have emerged from a burst of power at the climax of the 1960s.

There was much ballyhoo in the first years of the 1970s about Thompson's "breakthrough" to gonzo journalism. His Kentucky Derby piece in *Scanlan's* and the first few articles in *Rolling Stone* were daring. Their style seemed bold and innovative, and Thompson became one of the most talked-about writers of the era.

And yet those wild touches and flourishes that characterize his gonzo writing were there all along, even in his early work for the *National Observer*. It might be helpful to examine the body of Thompson's work as if it had a life of its own, to consider his first major publications the "birth" of this style, something like the birth of a child. At first, relatives cluster around the infant and argue about which of them the child most resembles. The young father sees only a baby—features have not yet formed. Yet fifteen or twenty years later, the father looks at a photograph of the infant and sees that the facial features that have blossomed in adulthood were present on the child's face all along. They were there, waiting to be awakened and noticed. Looking back on the early years of Thompson's style, it is now possible to see that the features distinguishing his writing were there all along, as were the features on the growing child's face.

Thompson's articles for the *Chicago Tribune*, the *Reporter*, the *National Observer*, and other newspapers fit into those publications. They fall within the traditions of each newspaper and do not appear to be radical. Yet they also bear indications of the wildness to come in another decade. Some of the phraseology and the cadence of the gonzo style are present in the work, waiting to be awakened and noticed.

A South American *Observer*

Thompson's best early association was with the *National Observer,* a publication started in 1962 as a "Sunday edition" of the *Wall Street Journal.* Barney Kilgore, the editor who lifted the *Journal* to greatness in the 1950s, was the driving force behind the establishment of the *Observer*. Kilgore saw the new venture aimed at young people who had not yet developed strong reading habits. Furthermore, he proclaimed that this newspaper would not need reporters. As Kilgore told the *Journal* staff at its 1961 editorial conference in Bermuda, "We don't need more people telling us what has happened as much as we need people who can put together events and explain them."[1] The publication he described sounded remarkably like *Time* magazine, and although the Dow Jones board of directors gave Kilgore the green light, the *Journal*'s reporters and editors were skeptical.

Yet Kilgore's gamble bore some fruit. During its ten-year life, the *Observer* was one of the most elegantly written and edited examples of American journalism. And Thompson was one of its first and farthest-flung correspondents, reporting from points of peril in South America. Thompson's early experience in journalism had shown him to be unable and unwilling to maintain the regimen of the daily newspaper grind. Yet he was obviously gifted at this type of writing, as even his press releases for the air force showed. After being fired from and/or quitting his various reporting jobs, Thompson decided to travel and lucked into this mutually beneficial association with the *Observer*. It allowed him to blossom and begin finding his style.

One characteristic of gonzo journalism that is apparent in these early *Observer* pieces is Thompson's participation in the story. Many of the articles emphasize his closeness to the action. After three paragraphs of Hemingwayesque introduction, "A Footloose American in a Smuggler's Den"[2] turns into a classic bit of comic Thompson. Upon arriving in a tiny Colombian village, the "first tourist in history" is greeted by the entire population of the village, "staring grimly and without much obvious hospitality." He had learned in Aruba that the men of this village wear neckties knotted just below the navel—and nothing else. "That sort of information can make a man feel uneasy," Thompson wrote, "and as I climbed the steep path, staggering under the weight of my luggage, I decided that at the first sign of unpleasantness I would begin handing out neckties like Santa Claus—three fine paisleys to the most menacing of the bunch, then start ripping up shirts."[3]

Thompson was lucky to be working for the *Observer*, which had not yet clearly defined its style. Although he sold occasional articles to mainstream publications, such as the *Chicago Tribune* and the *Boston Globe*,[4] his writing was too loose and ragged for most traditional newspapers, yet not structured enough for a slick magazine piece. The *Observer* allowed him to be methodical in his writing and slow to build to the point, as was the practice with the

Wall Street Journal's column-one features. Sometimes his pieces fit well within the *Journal* traditions. "Democracy Dies in Peru, but Few Seem to Mourn Its Passing"[5] is a long, detailed account of a military takeover of the Peruvian government. Though it contains first-person references, it is not in the more obtrusive style Thompson would adopt. In fact, this piece—with only a few alterations—would have been at home in the *Journal*.

But the *Observer* editors no doubt recognized Thompson's gifts and wanted to take advantage of them. His next major piece, in the end-of-the-year issue, exploited his quirky style. It was a collection of letters he had written to editors at the *Observer*, edited and (one assumes) censored for publication.[6] The editor's note said, "[T]here's another side to reporting that seldom shows up in formal dispatches—the personal experiences of the digging, inquisitive newsman. These often give fascinating insights on the land and the people."[7] In these letters to his editor, Thompson's gonzo begins, more obviously, to rear its head. His preoccupation with *getting the story* is now becoming the major part of the *story*. In one letter, datelined Quito, Ecuador, he writes: "I could toss in a few hair-raising stories about what happens to poor Yanquis who eat cheap food, or the fact that I caught a bad cold in Bogota because my hotel didn't have hot water, but that would only depress us both. As it is, I am traveling half on gall."[8] His casual tone works well in the *Observer*, as he begins a letter from Guayaquil, Ecuador: "Things are not going well here, my man." Later, from Lima, comes a passage that an archaeologist of journalism might regard as a find equivalent to Louis Leakey's finds in the Olduvai George. It may be the earliest species of gonzo journalism: "Some ***** has been throwing rocks at my window all night and if I hadn't sold my pistol I'd whip up the blinds and crank off a few rounds at his feet."[9] Much of the comfortable tone of these short pieces anticipates the tone of Thompson's later gonzo work, a just-between-us shared language of conspiracy that would mark his work with originality. Another short piece he wrote in that era is a brief evocation of tossing back beer on a tug in a South American river in 110-degree heat. In theme and tone, it reeks of later gonzo.[10]

Thompson's next two pieces were reversions to the approach he had used in previous articles. His account of a shooting at a nightclub in Rio de Janeiro is reminiscent of Ernest Hemingway's dispatches from the Spanish Civil War. Like Hemingway, Thompson refers to himself in the third person, to emphasize his closeness to danger without appearing to brag too much. Here is part of a Hemingway account: "They say you never hear the one that hits you. That's true of bullets, because if you hear them, they are already past. But your correspondent heard the last shell that hit this hotel.

He heard it start from the battery, then come with a whistling incoming roar like a subway train to crash against the cornice and shower the room with broken glass and plaster."[11]

Another Hemingway dispatch, written in the second person, presents Hemingway's rather cavalier attitude toward violence:

In the morning, before your call comes from the desk, the roaring burst of a high-explosive shell wakes you and you go to the window and look out to see a man, his head down, his coat collar up, sprinting desperately across the paved square. There is the acrid smell of high explosive you hoped you'd never smell again, and, in a bathrobe and bedroom slippers, you hurry down the marble stairs and almost into a middle-aged woman, wounded in the abdomen, who is being helped into the hotel entrance by two men in blue workmen's smocks. She has her two hands crossed below her big, old-style Spanish bosom and from between her fingers the blood is spurting in a thin stream. . . .

A policeman covers the top of the trunk, from which the head is missing; they send for someone to repair the gas main and you go in to breakfast. A charwoman, her eyes red, is scrubbing the blood off the marble floor of the corridor. The dead man wasn't you nor anyone you know and everyone is very hungry in the morning after a cold night and a long day the day before up at the Guadalajara front.[12]

Thompson's dispatch from Rio does not involve a war, yet his dispassionate description of the aftermath of violence at Domino, a nightclub, strongly evokes Hemingway's reporting from twenty-five years before. He refers to himself as an American journalist awakened by a 4:30 A.M. call from a friend, telling of the Brazilian army going wild in the streets in the Copacabana nightclub district of the city:

Ten minutes later the half-dressed journalist jumped out of a cab a block away from the action. He walked quickly, but very casually, toward the Domino Club, with his camera and flashgun cradled in one arm like a football. In a Latin American country nervous with talk of revolution, a man with good sense runs headlong into a shooting party, because he is likely to get stitched across the chest with Czech machine gun slugs.

But at 4:45 the Domino Club was quiet. It is—or was—a well-known clip joint, catering mainly to American tourists and wealthy Brazilians. The lure was girls— some young and pretty, others slightly piggy and painted after long years of service.

Now the Domino is a shell, a dark room full of broken glass and bullet holes. The doorman is dead; he was cut down by gunfire as he fled toward a nearby corner. The bartender is in the hospital with a bullet creased down the side of his skull, and several patrons are wounded. Most observers say another man is dead, but the bodies were taken away so quickly that nobody can be sure.[13]

The raid by the soldiers—in retaliation for the beating of one of their colleagues in the Domino a few weeks before—is described in graphic detail by Thompson, who barely conceals his outrage. At one point he even quotes himself, wondering what the reaction would be to a similar incident back home, were soldiers from Fort Knox to open fire in a Louisville night spot.

Thompson's next pieces covered Brazil's economic conditions after the nation's elections, and Bolivia's economic difficulties. A brief respite in the United States produced three articles for the *Observer*—devoted to a folk festival, horse racing, and the art of hitchhiking. His next piece from South America retraced the history of the Inca of the Andes,[14] noting that the wealth now was measured not in gold but in the sleeping political power of the Indians. It was a traditional piece, one that would have been appropriate for the opinion page of the *New York Times*. With the shooting story from Rio and the collection of "chatty letters," it made for a diverse series of articles by the *Observer*'s "roving South American correspondent," as the editor's notes characterized him.

Thompson's tenure in South America coincided with the era of "the ugly American," from Eugene Burdick's novel that portrayed the negative image of America in the third world. Thompson found much evidence of that ugliness, and it was not confined to his compatriots. He found the perfect paradigm in the image of an unfeeling Briton firing golf balls from a rooftop to the Colombian city below. In "Why Anti-Gringo Winds Often Blow South of the Border,"[15] he begins and ends his essay with that appalling image.

One of my most vivid memories of South America is that of a man with a golf club—a five iron, if memory serves—driving golf balls off a penthouse terrace in Cali, Colombia. He was a tall Britisher, and had what the British call "a stylish pot" instead of a waistline. Beside him on a small patio table was a long gin-and-tonic, which he refilled from time to time at the nearby bar.

He had a good swing, and each of his shots carried low and long out over the city. Where they fell, neither he nor I nor anyone else on the terrace that day had the vaguest idea. The penthouse, however, was in a residential section of the Rio Cali, which runs through the middle of town. Somewhere below us, in the narrow streets that are lined by the white adobe blockhouses of urban peasantry, a strange hail was rattling on the roofs—golf balls, "old practice duds," so the Britisher told me, that were "hardly worth driving away."[16]

Thompson's essay has some of the flavor of the best of Graham Greene's novels of the era—*Our Man in Havana* and *A Burnt-out Case*. It powerfully shows the displaced American or Briton in conflict with another culture. Some of the acts of callousness recall singer-songwriter Bob Dylan, whose work was meeting with acclaim at about the time Thompson was reporting from South America. Dylan became a great influence on Thompson, and *Fear and Loathing in Las Vegas* was dedicated to him. The "Anti-Gringo" story echoes Dylan's "The Lonesome Death of Hattie Carroll," a song Dylan based on news accounts of a Baltimore trial. William Zanzinger, a Maryland socialite, had recklessly twirled a cane that slipped from his hand and killed the housemaid, a black woman named Hattie Carroll. Thompson's outrage as he watches the golf balls loft into the poor residences of Cali matches Dylan's fury at the death of Hattie Carroll.

When a selection of Thompson's pieces for the *Observer* finally appeared in book form in *The Great Shark Hunt,* they were called "fair and straight-forward reports"[17] by the critics, who focused their reviews on the gonzo pieces and largely ignored the task of assessing Thompson as a "straight" reporter. But in fact the *National Observer,* despite its *Wall Street Journal* heritage, was one of the few publications in the country at the time that was loose enough to allow a rambunctious style like Thompson's to flourish.

Experiments in New Journalism

There were other fine publications, of course, and no shortage of rambunctious writers. While Thompson was chronicling the lives of drug smugglers in South America, Tom Wolfe, Gay Talese, and others were stretching the definitions of daily journalism in New York's major newspapers. They were all in competition, Wolfe said, to be the "best feature writer in town."[18] Talese, a reporter for the *New York Times,* began writing features for *Esquire* that redefined the celebrity interview. Reading Talese's story about former heavyweight boxing champion Joe Louis, Wolfe was awakened to the possibilities of what could happen when journalism used the techniques of the fiction writer. Talese's account of a weekend with Joe Louis was undoubtedly true, yet it read like a short story. There was little exposition, but mostly a presentation of scene-and-sequel.

Wolfe was a reporter for the *New York Herald Tribune.* Having earned a doctorate in American studies from Yale and reported for the *Washington Post,* he had landed in the *Herald Tribune* newsroom in 1962 in the middle of the great feature-writing competition in New York. All the writers were out to prove that they were the best feature writer in town. Most of them moonlighted and tried to pitch their articles to *Esquire,* which at the time was publishing some of the most innovative nonfiction writing in the country. Wolfe wangled an assignment from the *Herald Tribune* to do a story on a car rally in California. He sold *Esquire* on the story, giving them the assignment without the expense of funding the trip. Wolfe returned from California, wrote the piece for the *Herald Tribune,* but had a terrible time trying to write the *Esquire* piece:

At first, I couldn't even write the story. I came back to New York and just sat around worrying over the thing. I had a lot of trouble analyzing what I had on my hands. By this time, *Esquire* practically had a gun at my head because they had a two-page color picture for the story locked into the printing presses and no story. Finally, I told Byron Dobell, the managing editor at *Esquire,* that I couldn't pull the thing together. O.K., he tells me, just type out my notes and send them over and he will get someone else to write it. So, about 8 o'clock that night I started typing the notes out in the form of a memo that began, "Dear Byron." I started typing away, starting right with the first time I saw any custom cars in California. I just started recording it all, and inside of a couple of hours, typing along like a mad man, I could tell something was beginning to happen. By midnight, this memo to Byron was 20 pages long and I was still typing like a maniac. About 2 a.m. or something like that, I turned on WABC, a radio station that plays rock and roll music all night long, and I got a little more manic. I wrapped up the memo about 6:15 a.m., and by this time it was 49 pages long. I took it over to *Esquire* as soon as they opened up, about 9:30. About 4 p.m., I got a call from Byron Dobell. He told me they were striking out the "Dear Byron" at the top and running the rest of it in the magazine.[19]

Thus Tom Wolfe found his style, in an article titled "There Goes (Varoom! Varoom!) That Kandy-Kolored (Thphhhhhh!) Tangerine-Flake Streamline Baby (Rahghhh!) around the Bend (Brummmmmmmmmmmmmmmmmmm) . . . ." Wolfe's entry into the competition signaled the beginning of the revolution in journalistic writing that would take place in the 1960s. Wolfe soon became its historian, noting Fielding and Dickens as the major influences on the "New Journalists" and making his claim that journalism would become the new art form of the era. As modern antecedents, he noted John Hersey's *Hiroshima,* which documented the lives of six bomb survivors in the days after the blast, and Truman Capote's *The Muses Are Heard,* an account of an American troupe of *Porgy and Bess* on tour in the Soviet Union.

Yet the New Journalism as a form can be best dated from the early 1960s—with Talese, Wolfe, Jimmy Breslin, Terry Southern, John Sack, George Plimpton, and James Mills in the forefront. Eventually, Capote and Norman Mailer would come into the fold. It was a competition of the high-

est order—far beyond the best-feature-writer-in-town contests Wolfe said
lured him into the fray.

Thompson, who would become one of the major figures of New Journalism, was far removed from and to a large extent unaware of this new
form he was helping to define. While Wolfe and Talese were flexing their
muscles in *Esquire,* Thompson was thousands of miles away, on the front
lines in South America for the *National Observer.* He was part of a movement of whose existence he was largely unaware.

Back in the USA

Thompson returned to North America in mid-1963 and made a trip
back to Louisville, an event he turned into a musing on the city's racial
problems for the *Reporter.* Despite its subject—a journey home—
Thompson's piece was not personal in the way his *Observer* articles were. He
simply contrasted the public stance of official Louisville with the resentment
of the city's blacks, who said their reality clashed with the portrayal of race
relations offered by the city's clerisy.

He continued his association with the *Observer* for another year as its
roving correspondent, producing a score of articles, including several book
reviews. Given a free hand, Thompson chose to portray outsiders and
outcasts. He wrote about the leftover beatniks, American hitchhikers
(including himself; he claimed to have set the all-time distance record
for hitchhiking in Bermuda shorts), frustrated miners, deer hunters, the
beginnings of the Indian rights movement, and the last days of Ernest
Hemingway.

The Hemingway article grew from a pilgrimage Thompson made to the
writer's last home, in Ketchum, Idaho. The piece is part travelogue, part literary criticism, and part elegy, as Thompson delivers a benediction on the
writer-adventurer whose influence on his work was considerable: "Perhaps
he found what he came here for, but the odds are huge that he didn't. He
was an old, sick, and very troubled man, and the illusion of peace and con-
tentment was not enough for him—not even when his friends came up
from Cuba and played bullfight with him in the Tram. So finally, and for
what he must have thought the best of reasons, he ended it with a
shotgun."[20]

Thompson's *Observer* articles during this period are in many cases a rever-
sion to the standard techniques of journalistic feature writing. The adven-
turousness and the wild tone of the South American articles are subdued.
His article on Marlon Brando's attempt to help a group of Indians regain

their fishing rights in Washington[21] could easily be mistaken for an Associated Press Newsfeatures article of the era, although Thompson frequently began articles with unattributed quotes (as is the case with the Brando piece), a device most newspaper editors would strongly discourage.

Perhaps Thompson felt more constraints as he got closer to the *Observer* editors and the working relationship became more intense. Whatever the case, the tension between writer and editors was building, and as Thompson began to focus more of his articles on the San Francisco Bay Area, delivering a remembrance of the beatniks and bidding welcome to the hippies, the tensions grew intolerable. He quarreled with the editors over a piece on the free speech movement at the University of California at Berkeley in 1964, and he wrote his last article for the *Observer* in December of that year.

Thompson eventually published his account of the free speech movement in the *Nation,* the respected journal founded by Edwin Lawrence Godkin in 1865. The magazine's liberal audience no doubt found Thompson's sympathetic account of the disturbances in the Bay Area more palatable than the *Observer*'s more cautious copy editors would. Thompson's article nearly predicts the founding of radical organizations like the Weathermen, without, of course, offering time and date of charter. Yet his article, which appeared in 1965,[22] is prophetic in its speculation about where the students would go and the scope of the movement they were inspiring.

The association with the *Nation* was not long, but it was profitable. Editor Carey McWilliams had an assignment for Thompson that would allow the young writer to pull together a lot of his influences and attitudes. It grew from an article into his first book, a chronicle of the exploits of the outlaw motorcycle gang Hell's Angels.

Chapter Three
A Strange and Terrible Saga

Carey McWilliams, editor of the *Nation,* gave Thompson the assignment to write about the Hell's Angels motorcycle gang of the San Francisco Bay Area. The Angels had been the subject of a media blitz in 1965, earning cover stories in a variety of the country's top magazines, including the *Saturday Evening Post,* which alarmed its readers with tales of gang-bangs and orgies perpetrated by savage, long-haired motorcyclists. Several stories about rape charges lodged against the Angels kept the gang's saga on the front pages of major newspapers.

McWilliams was responding to this barrage of coverage when he asked Thompson to look into the real story of the Angels for the *Nation.* The resulting article[1] was the cover story of the magazine and brought the young writer much acclaim. One critic called it "probably the first piece of honest writing about the Angels done by any known journalist for a major publication."[2] Thompson had agreed to do the piece and had begun associating with the Angels when both *Time* and *Newsweek* hit the stands with extremely unflattering pieces about the motorcycle gang that "infuriated the outlaws and made them very hostile to anyone who claimed to be a reporter," Thompson recalled.

I recall some hairy moments from that era; there was talk of setting me on fire and whipping my head with chains. They wanted to teach the press a lesson and I was the only journalist they had access to.

After much drinking and shouting I convinced them that the *Nation* didn't share the same prejudices as *Time* and *Newsweek,* and that any article I wrote would be based on my own experience and not on rabid police reports.[3]

In the piece, Thompson takes aim at the journalism establishment, suggesting that reporters were contributing to a hysteria about the Hell's Angels. Journalists were shills for half-crazed law enforcers, spreading rumors and innuendos about the motorcyclists and filling the reading public with an unjustified fear. Remarkably—and paradoxically—Thompson simultaneously conveys his real sense of fear about the Angels.

Thompson indicates in his article that the Angels are symptomatic of something larger that is wrong with the country. They are a result, not a cause, of problems in American society.

They are, to the government and the press, easy targets. They are visible and noisy symbols atop their Harley-Davidsons and the government/media axis can focus a lot of public outrage on that symbol, Thompson writes. Legislation aimed at regulating motorclists in general and motorcycle gangs in particular is pointless. Thompson asks, "[W]ould it make any difference to the safety and peace of mind of the average Californian if every motorcycle outlaw in the state . . . were garroted within twenty-four hours?"[4] The Angels are outsiders and proud to proclaim themselves so. They engage in behavior that frightens a good many people, but actual violence is rare. After his brief glimpse into the Angels subculture for the article, Thompson is ready to dismiss the gang and open fire at the mainstream press—particularly *Time*, his former employer—for manufacturing and spreading the Angels rumors and for making a full-blown media event out of them.

He concludes the piece on a comic note, trying to make his point about big media to one of the Angels. The press, Thompson tells the outlaw, has such a vested interest in the establishment that it cannot delve deeply and honestly into the causes of unrest, and so it focuses on symbols such as the Angels, with their beards, long hair, swastikas, and roaring motorcycles. Yet the Angels shrug off Thompson's conspiracy theory about the press. As one member tells him, "[S]ince we got famous, we've had more rich fags and sex-hungry women come looking for us than we ever had before. Hell, these days we have more action than we can handle."[5]

Thompson's *Nation* piece, though somewhat shocking for its time with its raw language, still fit within the constraints of the classic journalistic feature article. It began with the dramatic opening (about a notorious rape case involving the Angels), followed the anecdote to its conclusion, then backpedaled for some time while Thompson cleverly wove background information into the narrative. He brought the story around to the rape case and dismissed it as the most grievous example of the media's inaccuracy in the rape case. The last segment, with the Angel who is pleased with the hordes of prospective new sexual partners, provided the perfect close to the piece. It was a masterful example of feature writing in which Thompson figured prominently as a character, but not to the extent that he would in his later journalism.

The Journalist as Daredevil

The article earned Thompson a name as a daredevil journalist for associating with the Angels. It also brought him a mailbox full of offers from publishers, lathering with hunger for a book-length treatment of the subject. All the stories in the mainstream press had been alarmist and written from the point of view of an outraged outsider; Thompson's was the first inside glimpse of the Angels subculture. After mulling over several of the proposals, Thompson signed an agreement with Random House when the publisher made an offer Thompson said he was "too broke to refuse."[6]

Taking encouragement from McWilliams, Thompson spent a year riding with the outlaws, and the resulting book was his first extended experiment with the participatory journalism that became his trademark in later years. Although a major part of the story, he was not the primary focus. In fact, he seemed distant by his later standards. He was not always center stage, though his presence was vital to the tone of the work. He shared the outrage of the earlier journalists—to some extent, at least—but the ever-resourceful Thompson was also ready to deal with the Angels on their level.

Several of the Angels accepted Thompson into the fold, yet he tried to maintain his distance as a writer. He would go on the gang's outings— "runs," as they were called—trying to dress so as not to be mistaken for one of them. Thompson was the first journalist to meet the Angels "on their own turf instead of relying on police information."[7] Some of the Angels became frequent uninvited guests at his apartment, dropping in with cases of stolen beer and drugs. These visits tested the tolerance and good nature of Sandy Thompson, who was horrified by her husband's involvement with the Angels.

The experience with the Angels was one of the most frightening episodes of his life, Thompson said. "Nobody can throw a gut-level, king-hell scare into you like a Hell's Angel with a pair of pliers hanging from his belt that he uses to pull out people's teeth in midnight diners," he said. "Some of them wear the teeth on their belts, too."[8] Thompson had impressed the Angels. He was a conventional-looking journalist from an elitist East Coast magazine who took the time to find them at a San Francisco transmission shop. They were initially taken aback, Thompson said, but after sharing six cases of beer, they felt at ease with him. They saw something in him that was familiar, he said. They saw that he, too, was a little crazy. He was also on the outside—an outlaw journalist.

Thompson credited growing up in racially divided Louisville and attending Male High School with preparing him well for his experience covering the Angels: "I suppose that three years in what was then the very mixed society of Male High taught me to get along with a lot of people I had not much in common with. Some Male grads of the 1950s went on to Princeton

. . . and a few I'm sure went to Eddyville [the state prison]. Among the people I knew in high school there were several who might have made good Hell's Angels."[9]

Using his advance from Random House, Thompson bought the fastest motorcycle that *Hot Rod* magazine had ever tested. But it was a BSA and the Angels rode only Harley-Davidsons. Despite this breach of etiquette, the Angels continued to let Thompson travel in their company, which he ended up doing for a full year. A few of the members asked him to join, but he refused to cross the line between journalist-participant and member-participant. He went on runs with them but did not dress like them, trying to tell them that he was a writer and had to retain the writer's distance. As a member, he would be bound by what he called the Angels' "brother thing" and would be unable to write about them honestly and candidly.

When Thompson found his deadline upon him ("screaming down . . . like a goddamn banshee"), he had to leave the Angels, find seclusion, and write—to "become the monster."[10] The monster did not rear his head prominently until near the end of the book. As *Hell's Angels* began, Thompson-as-a-presence was far below the surface. His presence in the book gradually intensified, until by the end, he was the focus for the brutal epilogue.

Hell's Angels

Hell's Angels begins with impressions, not even completely formed sentences, as Thompson depicts the fury of the Angels at the beginning of a run: "The Menace is loose again, the Hell's Angels, the hundred-carat headline, running fast and loud on the early morning freeway, low in the saddle, nobody smiles, jamming crazy through traffic and ninety miles an hour down the center stripe, missing by inches . . . like Genghis Khan on an iron horse, a monster steed with a fiery anus"[11] The burst of images is reminiscent of Tom Wolfe's early pieces, a comparison critic Michael L. Johnson made. He commended Thompson for his use of police reports, news reports, and epigraphs but said "it is his style that distinguishes the book as reportage and makes a New Journalistic work of art that reminds one of Wolfe, as it is probably influenced by him."[12]

Thompson quickly moves from the frightening images of the Angels in transit to the territory he had carved out in the *Nation* article: an attack on the mainstream press for its irresponsibility in presenting the Angels as a dire threat to society. Part of the significance of *Hell's Angels* was its assault on the traditional practice of journalism. Other works of New Journalism by Wolfe and Talese were revolutionary in their approach, in their style. *Hell's Angels* was also revolutionary in that sense, but in addition it was a full-frontal attack on the sensibilities of journalism. As Johnson wrote in *The New Journalism,* "Thompson's book is an especially significant document of the New Journalism, because it came about in large part because of his desire to correct the reportage of the established media, to get close to a way of life and write about it as it really is."[13]

Thompson begins gathering the evidence, using frequent epigraphs and often printing in their entirety scare stories about the Angels. This was the pattern Thompson would follow for much of his celebrated journalism, particularly writing about politics. Though working as a reporter and nursing at the breast of journalism, Thompson nevertheless has been an unrelenting critic of the press.

In *Hell's Angels,* he begins to define his practice of *reacting* to the press. The excerpts he quotes—from the *Saturday Evening Post, Time, Newsweek,* the *New York Times,* and so on—infuriate him, and his prose risks turning to screed as he picks apart the articles and attacks the journalists who write them. As Tom Wolfe wrote in *The Electric Kool-Aid Acid Test,* "[A]n amazing series of newspaper and magazine articles . . . had the people of the Far West looking to each weekend in the Angels' life as an invasion by baby-raping Huns."[14]

Often, in his later political writing, Thompson's vantage was not as good as it was in *Hell's Angels.* With the motorcycle gang, Thompson was a participant in or at least a witness to all that he was writing about. He was reacting to the misconceptions perpetrated by the press. In his political writing, he was more often reacting to events he had not witnessed.

Thompson finds the roots of the Angels' restlessness in the Great Depression. The Angels' ancestry frequently includes the men and women who had migrated to California from the Oklahoma dust bowl. He cites as a literary precursor Dove Linkhorn, the protagonist of Nelson Algren's 1956 novel, *A Walk on the Wild Side.* Like Linkhorn, most Angels were uneducated, were unemployed, and had no prospects—losers, pure and simple.

Thompson accompanies the Hell's Angels on their run to Bass Lake, California, over the Fourth of July weekend in 1965. He is there to witness the tensions between the motorcycle gang and the townspeople of the backwoods fishing community, and he uses his impressions to form the centerpiece of his book. This run comes during the peak period of publicity about the Angels as savage rapists pillaging the countryside. Tension is high, and many mainstream reporters are there to record the events at Bass Lake. Yet Thompson is on the inside, assisting the Angels in locating enough beer to get through the weekend, negotiating past police roadblocks. Despite all the coverage the Bass Lake trip earned, as Tom Wolfe noted, "only Thompson caught such overtones as the counterterror of the country boys with the ax handles who were just dying to lay waste the Hell's Angels right down to the last bone splinter, and the fever of the tourists who, far from fleeing the Angels, came to Bass Lake to watch them."[15]

Writing about that weekend, Thompson quickly sets up a scene ripe for confrontation, then steps back. He plays with the reader, dropping in seeming non sequiturs, yet always reminding his audience of the brooding terror in the background. The tensions are established in the first few paragraphs. Violence seems imminent. At one point during a confrontation, Thompson finds himself on a beer run for the Angels when he runs into a group of townspeople at the store, led by a "burr-haired honcho" with a pistol on his belt. Thompson asks why he is carrying the gun. " 'You know why,' he said. 'The first one of these sonsofbitches that gives me any lip I'm gonna shoot right in the belly.' "[16] The man asks Thompson what he is doing with them. Thompson replies that he is "only a journalist trying to do an honest day's work."

Then Thompson looks around and realizes he should take the situation more seriously: "The dusty street was so crowded with tourists that I hadn't noticed the singular nature of the group that surrounded us. They weren't tourists at all; I was standing in the midst of about a hundred vigilantes."[17]

Thompson does not dress like a Hell's Angel and on that trip to the store does not even ride a motorcycle. But he is identified as one by the crowd. A man in Bermuda shorts sidles up to him and asks, "Say, are you guys really Nazis?" "Not me," Thompson replies. "I'm Kiwanis."[18] Thompson manages to walk away from the scene at the store unscathed.

The Angels are the creation of the media, Thompson asserts, and they feed like piranhas on the free publicity. They had existed for eighteen years, but in six months went from obscurity to the covers of national magazines.[19] As Thompson becomes part of the Angels' milieu, he begins to see the comic spectacle of other (and presumably less worldly) journalists dealing with them. The Angels demand that other reporters pay them in order to have the pleasure of hanging around with them for a story. Yet they make no such demand of Thompson—at first. He begins hanging around with them to do the *Nation* piece in the spring of 1965. "By the middle of the summer," he writes, "I had become so involved with the outlaw scene that I was no longer sure whether I was doing research on the Hell's Angels or being slowly absorbed by them."[20]

If Thompson truly fears absorption into the world of the Angels, that fear evaporates after his severe beating at their hands. A group of gang members feel he is taking advantage of them, profiting off of them with his book. As he recalls: "I'd finished the book. Shit, the book was already in type. I didn't like the cover. I told Random House, 'You fucking pigs, I'll go out and photograph it myself.' It was a Labor Day run. I was showing the Angels the cover, and it said $4.95—whew, $4.95, that must have been a long time ago. And the Angels said, 'Jesus, $4.95! What's our share? We should get half.' And I said, 'Come on.' I was getting careless, see. I said, 'It takes a long time to write a book. Nothing—that's your share.' "[21]

And so they circle him, punch him, knock him down, and nearly kick him to death. One of his friends in the Angels breaks up the fight, which ends as suddenly as it begins. Bleeding profusely, spitting blood on the windshield, Thompson drives to a hospital emergency room and, while awaiting treatment, seeks an epitaph to his year with the Angels. All he can do is echo Joseph Conrad: "The horror! The horror! . . . Exterminate all the brutes!"[22]

"Talent" and "Courage"

Hell's Angels was published in spring 1967 to a great deal of acclaim, many of the reviews focusing on Thompson's "stunt" of riding with the outlaws. William James Smith, in *Commonweal,* called Thompson "a young man of considerable journalistic talent and no little personal courage since he spent a good deal of his time for a year or more in the company of the Hell's Angels and ended up being stomped by them."[23] Smith's review notes a tendency of Americans to romanticize their outlaws ("The homicidal maniacs of the Western Frontier become folk heroes pirouetting through ballets"), and Smith writes that a mythologizing of the Hell's Angels will not be long in coming, after publication of the book, although Thompson does his best to remove all romance from the gang.[24] Indeed, intellectuals at Berkeley had characterized the Angels as "a generation in revolt," perfect examples of alienated refugees from modern American society. Many Berkeley faculty members and local liberals had tried to use Thompson to meet the Angels, which was the hip thing to do in the Bay Area during that period.[25]

As Thompson himself noted in the wake of the book's publication, "One reviewer has called the book an 'ugly American document,' and I think I agree. The Hell's Angels are an ugly phenomenon; they are also an ominous symbol of something wrong at the roots of the society that breeds them. This is what I tried to write about; the Angels themselves were only a vehicle."[26]

Thompson's report made no pretensions of objectivity, since he was a participant in much of the action. But he did honor the journalistic ideal of sticking to the facts, as critic Leo E. Litwak noted in his *New York Times Book Review* piece on the book. Without ignoring the real antisocial and often dangerous behavior of the Angels, Thompson nevertheless methodically attacked the contentions of the California attorney general's report on the Angels that branded them as a public menace. He acquitted himself well as a pure reporter, immersing himself in the world of the Angels and telling the reader what he had seen. Litwak noted Thompson's "easy acceptance of violence," which gave the book a cartoon quality. "We observe the Angels brutalizing themselves and others and somehow we expect them to recover as quickly as a cartoon cat and mouse," Litwak wrote.[27]

Thompson earned some reputation as a celebrity for the book, even emerging as a character in Tom Wolfe's *The Electric Kool-Aid Acid Test,* a nonfiction novel about Ken Kesey. Wolfe's book came out the year after Thompson's and was seen as a major event in New Journalism. It underlined the differences between the writers, indeed between Thompson and the other celebrated practitioners of the new form. Thompson was in the story. He did not see how he could avoid being in the story. Wolfe, Truman Capote, Gay Talese, and the others made a point *not* to be in the story. They were writing from a third-person point of view, using the techniques of the novelist. Norman Mailer, who in *The Armies of the Night* wrote about his adventures during an antiwar demonstration, used the third-person point of view, referring to himself as "Mailer" or "the Beast."

Yet Thompson stubbornly used the first-person approach in *Hell's Angels* and has done so in everything since. He said that his work has to be written from that perspective because of the way he gathers information. He does not want to be the distanced observer that Wolfe can be, or to stand back to have the novelist's manipulative stance, as Capote did. Speaking of Wolfe, Thompson said:

See, Wolfe is not a participant. He's a hell of a reporter. But being part of the story is critical to me. Because that's where I get my interest in it. Wolfe gets his interest from backing off. And I get my interest from the adrenalin that comes from being that close. . . .

When Wolfe did the book on Kesey, he wasn't there for a lot of it. He re-created it. [Whistle of admiration.] I can't do that. It's too damn much work. It's easier to be there. Maybe it's more of a risk.[28]

And yet there is some ambiguity with regard to Thompson's role in the story. As one scholar observed, Thompson fills the function of a cultural interpreter. He has one foot in the mainstream of the society from which he comes, and the other foot mired in the subculture of the Hell's Angels. He is a "quasi-insider" in both these societies, a position that gives him a terrific advantage. He can convey the reality of the Angels' world as no traditional reporter (a representative of the mainstream) can, and yet he can tell the story that no member of the Angels would have the objectivity to articulate.[29]

In *Hell's Angels*, Thompson takes a stance as a new breed of cultural observer, an approach he would learn to adapt and exploit as the 1960s crested and he began his fascinating experiments with the form of journalism at the beginning of the 1970s.

Chapter Four
The Prince of Gonzo

Thompson's unique style came out of a disappointment. After *Hell's Angels,* Thompson went to work on a novel called *The Rum Diary,* which he has continued to tinker with for twenty years without publishing. Frustrated with the book, he kept the money coming in by writing a series of articles for such diverse publications as *Pageant* and *Playboy.* After writing a profile of skier-turned-huckster Jean-Claude Killy for *Playboy,* Thompson became incensed when the magazine rejected the piece as he had written it. In his anger he rewrote the piece and sent it to publisher Warren Hinckle, who ran it in the first issue of his new magazine *Scanlan's.*

The Killy article "failure" was perhaps one of the more fortuitous events of Thompson's career. The rewritten article for *Scanlan's* was a breakthrough of sorts for Thompson and the beginning of a short but influential association with the magazine. (Any association with the magazine was short; it lasted less than a year.) Thompson convinced Hinckle to fund a trip home to cover the Kentucky Derby, and the resulting piece saw the full flowering of Thompson's style in "The Kentucky Derby Is Decadent and Depraved." An acquaintance of Thompson's from his days covering the presidential campaign of 1968, Bill Cardoso of the *Boston Globe,* wrote Thompson after reading the Kentucky Derby piece, "That was pure Gonzo journalism."[1] Thus, Thompson's style finally had a name.

In both pieces, Thompson is a central character. Although "Strange Rumblings in Aztlan," his first major article for *Rolling Stone,* has some of the *National Observer* quality to it, it also relies heavily on Thompson's technique of metajournalism. Getting the story *is* the story.

These articles on Killy, the Derby, and the murder of a Chicano reporter appeared over a thirteen-month period, from March 1970 to April 1971. During that year, Thompson ran his high-profile but unsuccessful campaign for sheriff of Aspen. It would be difficult to think of a more critical time in his career as a writer and public figure, as his work and his personality garnered a great deal of media attention. All this served to set the stage for his masterwork, his "failed experiment" in gonzo journalism, which he wrote in late 1971. Soon, the term *gonzo* would appear in dictionaries. As critic Herbert Mitgang wrote in a review of Thompson's work, "Gonzo, his own brand of journalism, has even found its way into the new Random House dictionary, which uses such words as bizarre, crazy and eccentric to define it. No one else gets credit for Gonzo journalism in the dictionary; but then not many journalists would want it."[2]

Many critics have attempted to define gonzo, but few came up with a more pragmatic definition than John Filiatreau of Thompson's hometown newspaper, the *Courier-Journal*. Gonzo "can only be defined as what Hunter Thompson does," he wrote. "It generally consists of the fusion of reality and stark fantasy in a way that amuses the author and outrages his audience. It is Point of View Run Wild."[3] Gonzo requires virtually no re-writing, with the reporter and the quest for information as the focal point. Notes, snatches from other articles, transcribed interviews, verbatim telephone conversations, telegrams—these are elements of a piece of gonzo journalism.

"The Temptations of Jean-Claude Killy"

It is easy to see why the first of the three articles, "The Temptations of Jean-Claude Killy," was rejected by *Playboy*. Despite its nudity and its concern with "safe" radical issues, *Playboy* in the late 1960s was essentially conservative when it came to writing. Its articles were clearly establishment pieces, and the truly innovative journalism was appearing in *Esquire,* which had eliminated erotica in favor of New Journalism. When *Playboy* rejected his article, Thompson was livid. "That whole magazine is a conspiracy of anemic masturbators," he said. "Scurvy fish-fuckers to the last man. Like a gang of wild whores or inmates of some terrible pig house."[4]

Thompson's anger at the *Playboy* rejection is evident in the rewritten version as it appeared in *Scanlan's*. The sentences are filled with fury. Thompson had been assigned to do a trendy, slick-magazine profile on the champion skier and on the endorsements and other offers Killy received after winning three Olympic gold medals at Grenoble in 1968. But there were two problems with this plan: (a) Killy would not talk much, and (b) despite the public image being crafted for him, Killy was not a very interesting person.

Writing a straightforward profile of Killy would have made an excruciatingly dull piece of journalism. What Thompson did was make himself the centerpiece and write about his inability to develop a story from a superficial character.

From the start, Thompson is the focus. As would become his pattern in the early gonzo pieces, he has a confederate. In this case it is Bill Cardoso of the *Boston Globe.* Cardoso greets Thompson at Boston's Logan Airport, where he is supposed to be met by Killy. Immediately, however, the attention is on Thompson. Glancing at his attire, Cardoso notes that he looks like "a serious candidate for a drug bust."[5] Wearing jeans, a sheepskin vest, and love beads, Thompson stands out in the crowd at the airport and, later, at the motel where Killy is on view for ski-equipment dealers gathering for a regional convention. Thompson's arrival at the party brings the festivities to a screeching halt—not that that was hard to do. Thompson describes the scene as looking like "a cocktail party for the local Patrolmen's Benevolent Association."[6] Cardoso, in his Sancho Panza role, strolls around the dead party, mumbling to Thompson, "Jesus, where are we? This must be Nixon headquarters."[7] Snubbed by the ski salesmen because of his oddball appearance, Thompson ignores the traditional methods of writing profiles by openly insulting Killy's press agent and conducting short and surly interviews with the skier himself.

Thompson's piece was to concern itself with Killy's new career as a celebrity huckster. Retired from skiing at twenty-six, Killy was now endorsing Head ski equipment and making commercials for Chevrolet. In an extended scene at the Chicago Auto Show, Thompson contrasts performances by Killy and Chevrolet's other new pitchman, football great O. J. Simpson. Simpson is comfortable, a natural salesman. Killy, by contrast, comes across as patently insincere ("his voice was pure snake oil"),[8] extremely ill at ease singing the praises of cars he would not consider driving. Thompson reveals that Killy loathes not only Chevrolets but nearly everything about the United States. He plans to take the money and run.

Killy seems nearly emotionless until Thompson mentions the International Olympic Committee's concern about his endorsements and desire to strip him of his gold medals. Killy's temper flares, and Thompson sees there is something going on inside Killy's head; he is not merely a grinning mannequin. Indeed, Thompson conveys a good deal of sympathy and pity for Killy. He is trapped within an image he cannot tolerate; he does not have the freedom of being on the outside, as Thompson does. Thompson solemnly stands by, watching the grim spectacle of Killy enduring the handshaking falsity of salesmanship: "Chevrolet doesn't pay him to say what he thinks, but to sell Chevrolets—and you don't do that by telling self-righteous old men to fuck off."[9] Thompson, on the other hand, allows as how *he* has that freedom.

Thompson's description of the Chicago Auto Show is one of the best scene-by-scene constructions in his career to that point. Naturally, he must direct the focus on himself and contrast the garish automobile spectacular in the Stockyards Amphitheatre with his last journey to that venue—during the 1968 Democratic National Convention, when he had been beaten during the huge antiwar demonstration: "Chicago—this vicious, stinking zoo, this mean-grinning, Mace-smelling boneyard of a city; an elegant rockpile monument to everything cruel and stupid and corrupt in the human spirit."[10]

Thompson quickly dishes off the other characters in his piece. Simpson's "sales technique has all the subtlety of a power-slant on third and one. . . . O. J. *likes* this scene. His booming self-confidence suggests Alfred E. Neuman in blackface or Rap Brown selling watermelons at the Mississippi State Fair."[11] Gorging himself on the obscene spectacle, Thompson has a chance to have fun with the grinning dunces in the crowd:

Meanwhile, slumped in a folding chair near the Killy exhibit, smoking a pipe and brooding on the spooks in this place, I am suddenly confronted by three young boys wearing Bass Weejuns and Pendleton shirts, junior-high types, and one of them asks me: "Are you Jean-Claude Killy?"

"That's right," I said.

"What are you doing?" they asked.

Well, you goddamn silly little waterhead, what the hell does it *look* like I'm doing? But I didn't say that. I gave the question some thought. "Well," I said finally. "I'm just sitting here smoking marijuana." I held up my pipe. "This is what makes me ski so fast."[12]

Other characteristics of gonzo begin to emerge in the Killy piece. One is the mixture of fact with obvious fancy that is presented hush-voiced as fact. Discussing then–Chevrolet executive John DeLorean's efforts to secure successful pitchmen, Thompson reports, "Speculation that DeLorean was about to sign Allen Ginsberg proved to be false: General Motors doesn't need poets."[13]

Thompson also begins to define his political position as a gonzo journalist in this piece. Other journalists, with the somber reporting of what politicians and others in authority *say*, end up parroting the party line and preserving the myths, institutions, legends, and popular heroes of society. Thompson takes his stance as a destroyer of these and implies that gonzo is the truest form of journalism because it does not have to report what someone in authority says. In the Killy piece, Thompson strips the mask off of celebrity and shows what a sham the whole process can be. There is no truth in the economic system that Thompson describes. We also find Thompson taking shots at his colleagues in the straight press. At one point, he pulls Killy aside to ask some routine questions: "I reverted to a Hollywood-style of journalism that Killy instantly picked up on."[14]

Finally, we see Thompson's portrayal of himself struggling to bring his truth to the fore—against almost all odds. In this case, press agents want to use Killy's image to sell products. One shill who has done his best to keep Thompson away from Killy wants to discuss the photos that will accompany the article and ask that the Head ski logo be featured prominently in the picture. "Fuck the skis," Thompson tells him. "I couldn't give a hoot in hell if he skis on metal bowls; all I want is to talk to the man, in a decent human manner, and find out what he thinks about things."[15] But that, of course, is not part of the press agent's agenda. He wants to perpetuate the myth that Killy is a great lover, a great French sex symbol. That, however, proves not to be the case. But the press agents are so concerned with Killy's image that through innuendo they attempt to craft such an image for the client, hoping to mask the fact that he is actually quite dull. Thompson's frustration with his subject eventually erupts when he is talking to Killy on the telephone. "As far as I know," Thompson says to his subject, "you don't exist. You're a life-size dummy made of plastic foam. I can't write much of an article about how I once saw Jean-Claude Killy across a crowded room at the Stockyards Amphitheatre." After a pause, Killy laughs softly and says, "Well, maybe you could write about how hard it is to write about me."[16]

In his innocent way, Jean-Claude Killy had given Hunter S. Thompson the sense of mission he needed. "The Temptations of Jean-Claude Killy" was the necessary stepping-stone to the breakthrough three months later.

The Kentucky Derby

"The Kentucky Derby Is Decadent and Depraved" is the quintessential Hunter S. Thompson article. It is a flawless piece of work, as elegant and satisfying as a soufflé, despite its often-coarse subject matter and the supposed frenzy in which it is written. It is the best of the short-form version of gonzo. It is a spectacular example of the time when the self-indulgence and conceit that is gonzo paid off.

Unlike the Killy piece, there is a relatively clear statement of time with the Kentucky Derby article. Thompson chronicled his adventure from two days before the race until two days after. "Chronicled" may be a poor way to describe what he did, because his reality is punctuated freely with fantasy, as he describes what he would *like* to see happening.

From the moment of his arrival in Louisville, Thompson is conjuring up

visions of what the Derby is and what it means. He alarms "Jimbo," a
Derby fanatic from Houston, whom he meets in the airport lounge. Poker-
faced, Thompson informs Jimbo that he is a photojournalist from *Playboy*,
in town to cover the riot planned for Derby Day. In this opening scene,
Thompson uses italics a good deal to convey accent and inflection, showing
Jimbo and his comrades in their backslapping element: "By God! You old
bastard! Good to see you, boy! *Damn* good . . . and I *mean* it!" Alone with
Jimbo, Thompson grimly announces that the Black Panthers have been in
training for months for a massive riot at Churchill Downs. He calmly lets
Jimbo in on the news of the conspiracy, inviting his unwitting dupe into the
intelligence community. Horrified, Jimbo is stung as he sees a sacred American institution under attack:

"No!" he shouted; his hands flew up and hovered momentarily between us, as if to
ward off the words he was hearing. Then he whacked his fist on the bar. "Those
sons of bitches! God Almighty! The Kentucky Derby!" He kept shaking his head.
"No *Jesus!* That's almost too bad to believe!" Now he seemed to be sagging on the
stool, and when he looked up his eyes were misty. "Why? Why *here?* Don't they respect *anything?*"

I shrugged again. "It's not just the Panthers. The FBI says busloads of white
crazies are coming in from all over the country—to mix with the crowd and attack
all at once, from every direction. They'll be dressed like everybody else. You
know—coats and ties and all that. But when the trouble starts . . . well, that's why
the cops are so worried."

He sat for a moment, looking hurt and confused and not quite able to digest all
this terrible news. Then he cried out: "Oh . . . Jesus! What in the name of God is
happening in this country? Where can you get *away* from it?"

"Not here," I said, picking up my bag. "Thanks for the drink . . . and good
luck."[17]

The airport lounge scene seems too perfect, too good an introduction to
have simply occurred. It is one of those scenes that make Thompson's readers wonder about the ratio of fact to fiction in his writing. In his defense,
however, Thompson might offer William Faulkner's statement that "facts
and truth don't really have much to do with each other." Thompson may
occasionally drift from the letter of truth, but be true to its spirit.

Thompson, of course, is behind schedule. He does not have the proper
press credentials, and he does not know how to get in touch with his collaborator on the piece, an artist assigned by the magazine. As he recounts his
struggle to receive proper press credentials, he seems to be getting closer and

closer to a breakdown. He even threatens a Derby official in the press office with a blast of Mace.

He eventually tracks down Ralph Steadman, the English illustrator hired by *Scanlan's* to record the Derby. Steadman has never been to the United States before, and Thompson capitalizes on those virgin sensibilities, describing his fantasies to Steadman as he shows him around Churchill Downs:

"Just pretend you're visiting a huge outdoor loony bin," I said. "If the inmates get out of control we'll soak them down with Mace." I showed him the can of "Chemical Billy," resisting the urge to fire it across the room at a rat-faced man typing diligently in the Associated Press section. We were standing at the bar, sipping the management's Scotch. . . .

We had seats looking down on the finish line, color TV and a selection of passes that would take us anywhere from the clubhouse roof to the jockey room. The only thing we lacked was unlimited access to the clubhouse inner sanctum in sections "F&G" . . . and I felt we needed that, to see the whiskey gentry in action. The governor, a swinish neo-Nazi hack named Louie Nunn, would be in "G," along with Barry Goldwater and Colonel Sanders. . . .

This was the first time I'd been to a Derby in ten years, but before that, when I lived in Louisville, I used to go every year. Now, looking down from the press box, I pointed to the huge grassy meadow enclosed by the track. "That whole thing," I said, "will be jammed with people; fifty thousand or so, and most of them staggering drunk. It's a fantastic scene—thousands of people fainting, crying, copulating, trampling each other and fighting with broken whiskey bottles. We'll have to spend some time out there, but it's hard to move around, too many bodies."

"Is it safe out there? Will we ever come back?" [Ralph asked.]

"Sure," I said. "We'll just have to be careful not to step on anybody's stomach and start a fight." I shrugged. "Hell, this clubhouse scene right below us will be almost as bad as the infield. Thousands of raving, stumbling drunks, getting angrier and angrier as they lose more and more money. By midafternoon, they'll be guzzling mint juleps with both hands and vomiting on each other between races. The whole place will be jammed with bodies, shoulder to shoulder. It's hard to move around. The aisles will be slick with vomit; people falling down and grabbing at your legs to keep from being stomped. Drunks pissing on themselves in the betting lines. Dropping handfuls of money and fighting to stoop over and pick it up."[18]

The irony of the piece is that Thompson never sees what he expects to see. The race comes and goes without the spectacular orgy of excess for which he has so carefully prepared Steadman. To properly record the scene, of course, Thompson and Steadman make themselves into active participants in all the events, using the attendant drugs and alcohol. Thompson considers such absorption a critical part of his modus operandi. Throughout their journey, Thompson is constantly urging Steadman to find the "face"— the face that will encapsulate all the obscenity of middle America.

Tom Wolfe, writing about this piece, suggested that what saved Thompson from the usual excesses of first-person style was the way he portrayed himself—as a "frantic loser, inept and half-psychotic, somewhat after the manner of Céline."[19] Indeed, it is this self-deprecation carried to extreme that makes an article filled with such nastiness and rage ultimately charming. It is a technique that Thompson exploits—deflating his brutal criticisms with statements of his own prolific shortcomings.

Thompson's persistent fantasy is that he can lead Steadman to find the "face." He drags the artist through scene after scene at Churchill Downs, pointing out the garish and grotesque, urging that they be recorded. And yet the Derby comes and goes without seeing what Thompson had expected. And then Monday morning dawns:

Sometime around ten-thirty Monday morning I was awakened by a scratching sound at my door. I leaned out of bed and pulled the curtain back just far enough to see Steadman outside. "What the fuck do you want?" I shouted.

"What about having breakfast?" he said.

I lunged out of bed and tried to open the door, but it caught on the night-chain and banged shut again. I couldn't cope with the chain! The thing wouldn't come out of the track—so I ripped it out of the wall with a vicious jerk on the door. Ralph didn't blink. "Bad luck," he muttered.

I could barely see him. My eyes were swollen almost shut and the sudden burst of sunlight through the door left me stunned and helpless like a sick mole. . . .

My eyes had finally opened enough for me to focus on the mirror across the room and I was stunned at the shock of recognition. For a confused instant I thought Ralph had brought somebody with him—a model for that one special face we'd been looking for. There he was, by God—a puffy, drink-ravaged, disease-ridden caricature . . . like an awful cartoon version of an old snapshot in some once-proud mother's family photo album. It was the face we'd been looking for—and it was, of course, my own. . . .

[Later, at a nearby fast-food restaurant:]

By this time Ralph wouldn't even order coffee; he kept asking for more water. "It's the only thing they have that's fit for human consumption," he explained. Then, with an hour or so to kill before he had to catch the plane, we spread his drawings out on the table and pondered them for a while, wondering if he'd caught the proper spirit of the thing . . . but we couldn't make up our minds. His hands were shaking so badly that he had trouble holding the paper, and my vision was so blurred that I could barely see what he'd drawn. "Shit," I said. "We both look worse than anything you've drawn here."

He smiled. "You know—I've been thinking about that," he said. "We came down here to see this teddible scene: people all pissed out of their minds and vomiting on themselves and all that . . . and now, you know what? It's us."[20]

The Derby article was one of the first of what was to become a series of portrayals of the artist-as-beast. (Norman Mailer had done this with himself in *The Armies of the Night*). Indeed, Thompson's favorite epigram (and he is a writer who uses epigrams extravagantly) is from Samuel Johnson: "He who makes a beast of himself gets rid of the pain of being a man."[21] Thompson is himself what he expected to see at Churchill Downs: "And unlike most of the others in the press box, we didn't give a hoot in hell what was happening on the track. We had come there to watch the *real* beasts perform."[22]

As critic John Hellmann noted in *Fables of Fact: The New Journalism as New Fiction,* Thompson presents his facts through a distorted vision—the eyes of the drugged, burned-out narrator. This technique frees him to present journalistic material through "the licenses of parody." He can "flatten and warp" his presentation of reality because he has announced (more or less) that it is the product of a flattened and warped mind. Hellmann compares Thompson's persona/narrator to Chief Broom in Ken Kesey's *One Flew over the Cuckoo's Nest*.[23] In few places in Thompson's writing is this strong parody more evident than in "The Kentucky Derby Is Decadent and Depraved."

The reaction to the article was extremely positive from the New Journalism community. No one was more surprised than Thompson, who had thought the Derby piece would be the last article he would ever see published. Steadman quickly finished his drawings and sent them to Hinckle, and the magazine was set to go to press. "I was convinced I was finished," Thompson told an interviewer a few years later.[24] If Thompson is to be believed, he panicked while trying to complete the piece and sent Hinckle pages torn from his notebook. That approach is reminiscent of Tom Wolfe's scramble to finish "There Goes (Varoom! Varoom!) That Kandy-Kolored (Thphhhhh!) Tangerine-Flake Streamline Baby (Rahghhh!) around the Bend (Brummmmmmmmmmmmmmm). . . ."

After all the acclaim granted the article, Thompson said he swore off trying ever to be a "straight" journalist. Why try to write like the *New York Times* when he could write what he wanted and "get away with it"?[25]

Because of *Scanlan's* small circulation and its short life, the Derby article was one of the most famous and least read articles in Thompson's career. When it finally appeared nearly a decade later as part of the huge anthology

The Great Shark Hunt, critics considered it the highlight of that disjointed and seemingly disorganized book.[26]

"Strange Rumblings in Aztlan"

The final part of this early gonzo trilogy is the most serious piece of journalism Thompson had written since *Hell's Angels*. It also signaled the beginning of a profitable association with *Rolling Stone*. The magazine was only three years old, but it had quickly established itself nationally by discovering an audience interested in serious writing about rock and roll. The newsprint magazine soon broadened its scope to include other elements of the youth culture, or counterculture, as it was then known. One of those elements had been the bid by Thompson and his friends to take over Aspen. *Rolling Stone* gave the Freak Power movement national publicity. After that effort failed, Thompson drew an assignment from *Rolling Stone*'s young editor, Jann Wenner: he was to go to Los Angeles and investigate the relations between the white and Chicano communities.

"Strange Rumblings in Aztlan," though it again features Thompson as a prominent narrator, is basically a profile of crusading Chicano attorney Oscar Zeta Acosta, a character who speaks so much like Thompson that it might be tempting to label him an invention were his existence not well documented elsewhere. The article addresses the death of Ruben Salazar, a former *Los Angeles Times* reporter who had become news director of a Chicano television station in Los Angeles. Through a series of events that were never clearly explained, Salazar was killed after police officers raided a bar in an East Los Angeles barrio during a "Watts-like riot." The feeling among the Hispanic community is that it was deliberate, cold-blooded murder. In "Strange Rumblings," Acosta and his associates represent that point of view and take Thompson into their company.

Of course, Thompson becomes central to the story and the work of gathering information becomes the action of the piece. At a critical moment, the writer himself becomes the issue. Angry militants debate—in Thompson's presence—his value to them. He is allowed to associate with the militants but is never a close friend to any of them, except Acosta.

Though Thompson does not trust the powers-that-be in Los Angeles, he is dedicated to discovering the truth about Salazar's death, and sometimes his investigation leads him away from the course set by Acosta and the others. Even in a counterculture magazine in an era known for advocacy journalism, Thompson avoids the pitfalls of that genre. Despite his presence at center stage, Thompson is not swayed from the reporter's task of tracking down the truth, or something close to it. Thompson's respect and admiration for Acosta are obvious. But despite Thompson's concern with the inequities of Hispanic ghetto life in a white middle-class culture, he refuses to simply parrot Acosta's account of Salazar's death.

Along the way, the writer stops to take some of his usual shots, including a swipe at the *Los Angeles Herald-Examiner,* "a genuinely rotten newspaper that claims the largest circulation of any afternoon daily in America. As one of the few remaining Hearst organs, it serves a perverted purpose in its role as a monument to everything cheap, corrupt and vicious in the realm of journalistic possibility."[27]

And again, Thompson portrays himself as a troublemaker, a screwup, the "frantic loser" that Wolfe described: "It was difficult, even for me, to believe that the cops had killed him deliberately. I knew they were capable of it, but I was not quite ready to believe they had actually done it . . . because once I believed that, I also had to accept the idea that they were prepared to kill anybody who seemed to be annoying them. Even me."[28]

The Salazar piece would make a good case study for a class of journalists-in-training. Despite the tension between the Chicano community and the police and despite the well-founded suspicions of his militant associates, Thompson refuses to accept the notion of a murder planned at the highest levels of Los Angeles municipal government. The police department issues several versions of the event, methodically discounted by eyewitnesses; the militants suggest that these cover stories validate their accounts. Yet Thompson remains the skeptical journalist, in part *because of* the ever-changing cover stories from the police. In the end, he concludes:

Ruben Salazar couldn't possibly have been the victim of a conscious, high-level cop conspiracy to get rid of him by staging an "accidental death." The incredible tale of half-mad stupidity and dangerous incompetence on every level of the law enforcement establishment was perhaps the most valuable thing to come out of the inquest. Nobody who heard that testimony could believe that the Los Angeles county sheriff's department is capable of pulling off a delicate job like killing a newsman *on purpose*. Their handling of the Salazar case—from the day of his death all the way to the end of the inquest—raised serious doubts about the wisdom of allowing cops to walk around loose on the street. A geek who can't hit a 20 foot wide ceiling is not what you need, these days, to pull off a clean first-degree murder.[29]

"Strange Rumblings in Aztlan" showed the effectiveness of Thompson's "open notebook, no rewriting" approach in the setting of a traditional journalistic article. Though the author was the focus, the article showed him executing an impressive piece of detective work, as a more conventional investigative reporter would do. By offering the reader his prejudices, Thompson ensures that all biases are open and honest. They may also be unjustified, as some have suggested. In a brief passage about Chicano heritage, Thompson evokes memories of the Alamo, which bears not at all on the experience of California Hispanics but on that of Texas Hispanics. One critic noted, "As usual, Thompson is barely interested in facts."[30] Thompson might shrug in reply that he never let the facts get in the way of a good story.

These three articles are critical in the development of Thompson's gonzo journalism. They put him—and the publications in which they appeared—on the map in the early 1970s. With such a forum and a growing reputation, Thompson was ready to present gonzo in full flower.

Chapter Five
Rolling Stoned

Thompson's first association with *Rolling Stone* was as the subject of an article about his campaign for sheriff in Aspen, Colorado. Thompson's celebrated but unsuccessful fling with elective politics created a stir when it was publicized in the San Francisco–based magazine. After his bid failed, he began writing for the magazine's editor, Jann Wenner, whom *Parade* called the "young publishing genius" and who the *Columbia Journalism Review* said had "spoken for—and to—an entire generation of young Americans."[1]

Wenner was often in the company of eccentric rock-and-roll stars during a particularly strange time in popular-music history, but even he was startled by Hunter Thompson when the writer appeared in the magazine's office one afternoon. Thompson was there to get some national publicity for his candidacy. After Wenner got over the surprise of Thompson's bewigged appearance and abrupt manner, he became entranced by the man.

Wenner thought his magazine was in trouble. Though it was closely tied to popular music, such music was in a rather dull period: the Beatles had broken up, Bob Dylan was reclusive, and the Rolling Stones were licking their wounds after their disastrous free concert in Altamont, California, at which a spectator was murdered in front of the stage; no other artists were filling the void created by the absence of those giants. So Wenner wanted something new for the magazine. Others on the staff had been trying to move *Rolling Stone* in the direction of radical politics, but Wenner had vigorously resisted doing so. Yet an article about the Freak Power campaign seemed a worthy idea to Wenner. It was radical, but it was also comic—particularly Thompson's platform, which Wenner printed verbatim as a sidebar to the story on the campaign. The reaction to the story was positive, and Wenner decided to employ Thompson to write a longer piece for the magazine.

"Strange Rumblings in Aztlan" was an impressively detailed article—perhaps the first piece of serious journalism published by the magazine that had nothing to do with music. Previously, nonmusic stories had been political polemics, horribly slanted and amateurishly written. Thompson, however, was skilled as a writer and, unlike most radical writers, admitted an honest, open bias. The article was an immense success and Wenner wanted more.

As noted earlier, the piece on Ruben Salazar led Thompson to attorney Oscar Zeta Acosta, and they became fast friends. Acosta would figure heavily in Thompson's next article for *Rolling Stone,* which was, in Thompson's words, a "failed experiment" in gonzo journalism, yet also the masterpiece of the form. It first appeared as a two-part article in *Rolling Stone,* published under the byline "Raoul Duke." By the time it appeared in book form in the spring of 1972, Thompson had reinstated his name on the work.

This was *Fear and Loathing in Las Vegas,* which began as an assignment to provide a few hundred words to serve as caption information for a photo essay on the Mint 400 motorcycle race in Las Vegas for *Sports Illustrated.* Thompson was working with Acosta on the Salazar piece and finding it difficult to speak with the attorney with his associates present; the militants did not think Acosta should associate with a gringo. Thompson took Acosta to the Beverly Hills Hotel so that they could have some time together to talk, away from the distrusting associates. Sitting on the hotel patio, having a drink during the first calm moment in several weeks, Thompson remembered something a friend of his had said recently. The friend worked for *Sports Illustrated* and had asked him if he wanted to go to Las Vegas and do some minimal reporting on a motorcycle race. Thompson had been too immersed in the details of the murder of Ruben Salazar to respond when he had been asked. But now, having worked on the Salazar story and needing time with Acosta, he looked on the Vegas assignment as the perfect opportunity to get away from Los Angeles and its distractions and to have some time to really talk with Acosta. Thompson thus called *Sports Illustrated* and took the assignment.

He eventually sent the magazine twenty-five hundred words, which proved to be rather long for a copy block. Thompson said the manuscript was "aggressively rejected," and *Sports Illustrated* refused to pay even his minimum expenses.[2] While in Las Vegas, Thompson worked on the Salazar article. Acosta had to return to California, and Thompson tried to pull together the piece, which was running to nearly twenty thousand words. He would work all night, then unwind for an hour or so each dawn, working on a journal of his trip to Las Vegas. Wenner, hearing that Thompson was in Las Vegas, suggested that he cover the National District Attorneys Association's Third Annual Institute on Narcotics and Dangerous Drugs, being held at Caesar's Palace. Acosta returned to accompany the journalist to some of the sessions.

While Thompson labored in his hotel suite, running up a bill he knew he could not pay, he felt he was in the grip of "the Vegas thing," as he called it. He returned to Los Angeles and did further work on the Salazar article, managing to spend an hour or so each morning working on the Las Vegas project as well. When he went to San Francisco to deliver the manuscript of "Strange Rumblings in Aztlan" to Wenner, he showed Wenner the five thousand words he had pulled together about the Las Vegas adventure. Wenner liked the material enough to set a publication date for it in *Rolling Stone,* and that action gave Thompson the deadline he needed to finish it. As with *Hell's Angels,* the last part of the book was written at a frantic pace.

A "Failed Experiment"

Fear and Loathing in Las Vegas was Thompson's first sustained and conscious attempt to write gonzo journalism. He called the book a "failed experiment" because it violated one of the basic tenets of gonzo: no revision. Gonzo was to be first-draft, written-at-the-moment. The finished book has a genuinely spontaneous feel, and Thompson worked hard to keep the gonzo flavor in the work as he wrote and rewrote. He said he imposed a fictional framework on what had begun as a piece of journalism.

(A decade later, Thompson seemed to have had second thoughts about the first-draft nature of gonzo journalism. In an interview with the Associated Press, he said, "I've never really sat down and done what I should do. I haven't done a second draft of anything since 'Vegas,' and it might be interesting to see what would happen if I did."[3] So the business about the books being a "failed experiment" may be a self-serving reference to what Thompson conceives to be his abilities when he makes a serious effort.)

In terms of his prospectus, Thompson's work differs little in its ambition from the works of Tom Wolfe. Thompson has said "fiction" and "journalism" are inherently artificial categories, and he seems to have taken it upon himself to further blur the distinction. Indeed, it is amusing to see where libraries shelve *Fear and Loathing in Las Vegas.* Some classify it as nonfiction, modern history, or sociology. Others place it with novels. And still others consider it a travelogue—although it might frighten off would-be vacationers to Las Vegas.

Thompson was not at all modest about the book and was eager to admit that he liked it, even though he had failed in his mission. Discussing the work, he made one of his few attempts to define gonzo journalism:

My idea was to buy a fat notebook and record the whole thing *as it happened,* then send in the notebook for publication—without editing. That way, I felt the eye and mind of the journalist would be functioning as a camera. The writing would be selective and necessarily interpretive—but once the image was written, the words would be final; in the same way that a Cartier-Bresson photograph is always (he says) the full-frame negative. No alterations in the darkroom, no cutting or cropping, no spotting . . . no editing.

. . . True Gonzo reporting needs the talents of a master journalist, the eye of an artist/photographer and the heavy balls of an actor. Because the writer *must* be a participant in the scene, while he's writing it—or at least taping it, or even sketching it. Or all three.[4]

Thompson made the distinction that separated him from other New Journalists: his insistence that he be a participant, that he be the focus of the story. Norman Mailer's adventures in journalism often put him at center stage, yet his tremendous ego was offensive and obtrusive. Thompson, on the other hand, was modest and self-deprecating at the same time he was being a mad-dog journalist—an interesting and intoxicating combination, and difficult to pull off. Tom Wolfe and Gay Talese, other prominent New Journalists, were too standoffish for Thompson's tastes. Thompson criticized Wolfe for being too crusty to participate in his stories. "The people he feels comfortable with are as dull as stale dogshit," Thompson wrote, "and the people who seem to fascinate him as a writer are so weird that they make him nervous."[5] Thompson was one such person. He appeared as a character in Wolfe's *The Electric Kool-Aid Acid Test,* the book about writer Ken Kesey and his strange psychedelic voyage through the 1960s.[6] Wolfe's book was a remarkable chronicle of that outrageous decade; Thompson's *Fear and Loathing in Las Vegas* served as the perfect coda to the 1960s experience.

In Thompson's notes on the writing of book, which were not published for nearly a decade, he said that for him, one of the most notable things about the experience was that the book had been fun to write. This aspect startled him. "I've always considered writing the most hateful kind of work," he wrote. "Nothing is fun when you *have to do it.* . . . So it's a rare goddamn trip for a locked-in, rent-paying writer to get into a gig that, even in retrospect, was a kinghell highlife fuckaround from start to finish . . . and then to actually get *paid* for writing this kind of manic gibberish seems genuinely weird; like getting paid for kicking Agnew in the balls."[7]

Whether fact or fiction, the book certainly *reads* like fiction; therefore, a detailed summary of the plot appears to be in order.

Making a Beast of Himself

Thompson dedicates *Fear and Loathing in Las Vegas* to Bob Dylan, for his song "Mr. Tambourine Man," and cites Johnson's epigram "He who makes a beast of himself gets rid of the pain of being a man." Thompson's characters—Raoul Duke and "Dr. Gonzo," his permutation of Oscar Acosta—do make beasts of themselves, from the note-perfect beginning of the book through the end of the wild ride:

We were somewhere near Barstow on the edge of the desert when the drugs began to take hold. I remember saying something like "I feel a bit lightheaded; maybe you should drive. . . ." And suddenly there was a terrible roar all around us and the sky was full of what looked like huge bats, all swooping and screeching and diving around the car, which was going about a hundred miles an hour with the top down to Las Vegas. And a voice was screaming: "Holy Jesus! What are these goddamn animals?"

Then it was quiet again. My attorney had taken his shirt off and was pouring beer on his chest to facilitate the tanning process. "What the hell are you yelling about?" he muttered, staring up at the sun with his eyes closed and covered with wraparound Spanish sunglasses. "Never mind," I said. "It's your turn to drive." I hit the brakes and aimed the Great Red Shark toward the shoulder of the highway. No point mentioning those bats, I thought. The poor bastard will see them soon enough.[8]

Armed with a trunkload of drugs—including marijuana, mescaline, LSD, cocaine, pills, amyl nitrates, ether, tequila, rum, and beer—Duke and Gonzo (now a three-hundred-pound *Samoan* attorney) make beasts of themselves in Las Vegas. Perhaps spoofing, perhaps serious, Thompson cloaks this madcap adventure in the guise of looking for the American dream, which was a pursuit common in the pop art of the era—witness *Easy Rider* and other artifacts of the youth genre. Perhaps Thompson offers this search as a valid theme. Perhaps his drug-numbed tongue is in his cheek. He leaves the reader to decide.

Early in the book, Duke and Gonzo pick up a young hitchhiker, a "poor Okie kid" who admits he has never been in a convertible before. "We're your friends," Dr. Gonzo smiles at the boy. "We're not like the others." Duke is worried that his attorney has gone round the bend. "No more of that talk," he tells him, "or I'll put the leeches on you." Duke is in such a drugged state that he cannot tell the difference between what he is saying and what he is just thinking. He feels the need to tell the boy what he is up to. "[I] want you to know that we're on our way to Las Vegas to find the

American Dream," Duke tells the boy. Renting the enormous convertible was necessary in order to pursue this quest. Duke recounts the story of sitting in the hotel bar when the urge to go to Las Vegas struck. Duke raves: "This is the American Dream in action! We'd be fools not to ride this strange torpedo all the way out to the end." With his attorney in tow, he gathers the drugs, rents the car, and takes off on the trip. Yet he is unable to articulate clearly how Las Vegas will in some way embody the American dream. He drops off the hitchhiker alongside the road, in the desert, frustrated and as bewildered as the boy.

Soon after Duke and Gonzo's arrival in Las Vegas and their attempts to check into the hotel, Duke is hallucinating. The massive ingestion of LSD has caused him to see huge alligators and lizards all around him—the people have turned into reptiles. Gonzo is not entirely sympathetic:

"Look outside," I said.
   "Why?"
   "There's a big . . . machine in the sky . . . some kind of electric snake . . . coming straight at us."
   "Shoot it," said my attorney.
   "Not yet," I said. "I want to study its habits."[9]

Gonzo rails at Duke for his hallucinations and ravings during the check-in, but of course he is too sensitive. In the madness of Las Vegas, Duke's behavior had been virtually unnoticed or passed off as "mere drunkenness." Although thoroughly drugged, the two blend in with the race participants and spectators and use the opportunity to make genuine and demented sport. Driving around the desert in a press vehicle, they encounter two dune buggies full of "what looked like retired chief petty officers from San Diego," looking for the race. They ask Duke where the racers are. "Beats me," he tells them. "We're just good, patriotic Americans like yourselves." He notes their buggies covered with flags and other symbols of American might. He decides to have sport at the expense of the reporters in the press vehicle up ahead of them. He tells the chief petty officers that if they want a good chase, they should "get after that skunk from CBS News" in the car in front of them. "He's the man responsible for *The Selling of the Pentagon*," Duke tells them. " 'Hot damn!' two of them screamed at once. 'A black jeep, you say?' "[10]

The race, of course, bores them, and so Duke and Gonzo decide to do their best to terrorize Las Vegas and see if anyone will notice. They bull their way into a Debbie Reynolds show at the Desert Inn, where the entertainer is prancing onstage in a silver Afro wig, gyrating to the big-band sound of "Sgt. Pepper's Lonely Hearts Club Band." "Jesus creeping shit!" Gonzo yells. "We've wandered into a time capsule."[11] Ejected from the hotel, they manage to blend in with the carnalities of Las Vegas at Circus-Circus, a combination casino and big-tent show:

Right above the gaming tables the Forty Flying Carazito Brothers are doing a high wire trapeze act, along with four muzzled Wolverines and the Six Nymphet Sisters from San Diego . . . so you're down on the main floor playing blackjack, and the stakes are getting high when suddenly you chance to look up, and there, right smack above your head is a half-naked fourteen-year-old girl being chased through the air by a snarling wolverine, which is suddenly locked in a death battle with two silver-painted Polacks who come swinging down from opposite balconies and meet in mid-air on the wolverine's neck.[12]

It is too weird, even for Duke and Gonzo. "I think I'm getting the fear," the attorney says. "Nonsense," Gonzo responds. "We came out here to find the American Dream, and now that we're right in the vortex you want to quit. . . . You must *realize* that we've found the main nerve."[13]

They continue their quest for the elusive American dream through casino after casino, and eventually they run afoul of the management. Gonzo leaves town, catching the first plane he can back to Los Angeles. Duke becomes a virtual prisoner in his room, unable to pay the bill, unable to leave. Eventually a telegram arrives from Gonzo, announcing a new assignment from *Rolling Stone,* to cover a conference on drug abuse. Duke does not believe the message and sets off through the desert, pointing the nose of his Great Red Shark toward Los Angeles. He gets pulled over by the highway patrol, and despite driving at speeds in excess of a hundred miles an hour, with an open beer in his hand, he is let go with only a warning. He stops at a phone booth in the desert and calls Gonzo back in Los Angeles. Get back to Las Vegas, Duke is told. The assignment was real. Duke decides that this must be the American dream—getting paid for running amok.

Back in Las Vegas, Duke exchanges the Great Red Shark for the White Whale—a Cadillac convertible—and goes to the Flamingo, where *Rolling Stone* has reserved a suite for his use. It is the home hotel of the drug convention, and so the lobby is filled with cops waiting impatiently as they try to straighten out their room arrangements. The situation is too much to resist, and Duke decides to do what he can to mess with a *roomful* of authority:

So I stepped around the Pig and spoke directly to the desk clerk. "Say," I said, "I hate to interrupt, but I have a reservation and I wonder if maybe I could just sort of slide through and get out of your way." I smiled, letting him know I'd been digging his snake-bully act on the cop party that was now standing there, psychologically off-balance and staring at me like I was some kind of water-rat crawling up the desk.

I looked pretty bad: wearing old Levis and white Chuck Taylor All-Star basketball sneakers . . . and my ten-peso Acapulco shirt had long since come across at the shoulder seams from all that road-wind. My beard was about three days old, bordering on standard wino trim, and my eyes were totally hidden by Sandy Bull's Saigon-mirror shades.

But my voice had the tone of a man who *knows* he has a reservation. I was gambling on my attorney's foresight . . . but I couldn't pass a chance to put the horn into a cop.[14]

It was infuriating to the police officers, to be upstaged by (as Duke calls himself) a "crusty drifter," and Duke took enormous pleasure in sliding by them.

Thompson was prepared for the drug-abuse conference. Covering the motorcyle race had been boring, he said, because it had required only observation. The drug-abuse conference would require participation. The law enforcement community had descended on Las Vegas to face the Drug Menace, and Duke and Gonzo *were* the Drug Menace in the sweaty flesh. "If the Pigs were gathering in Vegas for a top-level Drug Conference," Duke thought, "we felt the drug culture should be represented."[15]

Duke was looking forward to the prospect of the fun he could have at the conference, until he checked into his room and found that Gonzo had preceded him. The attorney had brought a teenage girl into the suite with him—an apparently drug-addled, angry young woman "with the face and form of a Pit Bull."[16] Dr. Gonzo was nude, grinning lasciviously. "This is Lucy," he tells Duke. "You know—like Lucy in the sky with diamonds."

The Lucy episode is one of the more manic and frightening sections of the book. Lucy is a nearly mute young woman from Montana who amuses herself painting portraits of Barbra Streisand, portraits that show "teeth like baseballs, eyes like jellied fire." Her plan is to present the portraits to La Streisand Herself. But the singer is not in town—as Lucy and Gonzo believed she was—and will not open her engagement in Las Vegas for another three weeks. Duke hatches a plan to make Lucy over into a prostitute for the benefit of the visiting law enforcement officials. As he tells Gonzo, "These cops will go fifty bucks a head to beat her into submission and then gang-fuck her. We can set her up in one of these back-street motels, hang pictures of Jesus all over the room, then turn these pigs loose on her. . . . Hell, she's strong; she'll hold her own."[17]

Duke convinces Gonzo to abandon Lucy. They take her to the airport and give a skycap ten dollars to make sure she gets to the Americana Hotel somehow. She is incoherent, and Duke and Gonzo think they have seen the last of her. But when they get back to their room, there is a message from Lucy. Duke hangs up on the room clerk who informs him of the message. But the room clerk calls back a moment later, thinking they had been cut off. He repeats the message, but Duke is furious, sputtering into the phone:

"We're watching the news," I screamed. "What are you interrupting me for?"
Silence.
"What do you *want?* Where's the goddamn ice I ordered? Where's the booze? There's a war on, man! People are being killed!"
"Killed?" he almost whispered the word.
"In Vietnam!" I yelled. "On the goddamn television!"
"Oh . . . yes . . . yes," he said. "This terrible war. When will it end?"[18]

The room clerk wanted to inform Duke—since he had checked in as an investigator in Las Vegas for the drug convention—that the woman who called sounded "very disturbed." Duke tells the clerk that Lucy is their case study, a statement that seems to ward off the menace of being caught. Duke then threatens to leave unless Gonzo deals with the Lucy issue. Accordingly, the attorney calls her, talks briefly, then throws down the receiver and fakes the sounds of a violent scuffle with police authorities. The scene he creates is intended to lead Lucy to believe the police will find her at her hotel. He screams, then slams down the phone and smiles smugly. "That's that," he tells Duke. "She's probably stuffing herself down an incinerator about now."[19]

Gonzo introduces Duke to a new drug—adrenochrome, which comes from the adrenal glands of a living human body. They take the drug and watch President Nixon addressing the nation on television. But their minds are so blurred that the only word Duke can make out is "sacrifice . . . sacrifice . . . sacrifice."

The drug convention finally gets under way in a huge ballroom at the hotel. Duke and Gonzo sit amid the packed crowd of law enforcement officials, their heads spinning from the effects of adrenochrome and mescaline. At the distant podium, a speaker, a so-called expert, is informing the ignorant audience about the drug culture. Introducing the crowd to the language of drugs, the speaker says that a marijuana cigarette is called a roach because it resembles a cockroach. Gonzo leans over to Duke and says, "You'd have to be crazy on acid to think a joint looked like a goddamn cockroach." Indeed, as Duke observes, those charged with enforcing the drug-abuse laws are ignorant of that evil which they are supposedly monitoring. The speaker discusses the "four states of being" in the drug culture—"Cool, Groovy, Hip and Square"—and is so lame and utterly removed from reality that Duke nearly loses control.

Duke and Gonzo, who had decided to pose as undercover narcotics investigators, are dressed rather conservatively to blend in with the crowd. But the sessions are so tiresome that they soon lose patience, and the pleasure of watching people make idiots of themselves wears thin. The irony, of course, is great: here is an audience of police officers and district attorneys yammering about the evils of drug abuse, and sitting among them are two frequent and prolific abusers. But there is no risk. As Duke observes, "These poor bastards didn't know mescaline from macaroni."[20]

Duke muses that perhaps he could have attended the convention while using LSD rather than mescaline, but

there were faces and bodies in that group who would have been absolutely unendurable on acid. The sight of a 344-pound police chief from Waco, Texas, necking openly with his 290-pound wife (or whatever woman he had with him) when the lights were turned off for a Dope Film was just barely tolerable on mescaline—which is mainly a sensual/surface drug that exaggerates reality, instead of altering it—but with a head full of acid, the sight of two fantastically obese human beings far gone in a public grope while a thousand cops all around them watched a movie about the "dangers of marijuana" would not be emotionally acceptable.[21]

These thousand cops were telling one another that they needed to come to terms with the drug culture, but as Duke said, they "couldn't even *find* the goddamn thing." In the hotel bar, Duke and Gonzo terrorize their fellow customers with tales of drugs and crime and say that new Charles Mansons are everywhere, under every rock. Out on a cruise down the Las Vegas strip, Duke and Gonzo terrorize the tourists, offering heroin to two cop couples in a convertible pulled up at the stoplight next to them. In a bar, Duke surveys the crowd: "These are people who go absolutely crazy at the sight of an old hooker stripping down to her pasties and prancing out on the runway to the big beat sound of a dozen 50-year-old junkies kicking out the jams on 'September Song.' "[22]

At one point, the narrative breaks down and a transcript of Duke's tape is offered as the contents of one chapter. Now in suburban North Las Vegas, Duke and Gonzo stop at a taco stand to ask directions:

Att'y: . . . We're looking for the American Dream and we were told it was some-where in this area. . . . Well, we're here looking for it, 'cause they sent us out here all the way from San Francisco to look for it. That's why they gave us this white Cadillac, they figure we could catch up with it in that. . . .

Waitress: Hey Lou, you know where the American Dream is?

Att'y (to Duke): She's asking the cook if he knows where the American Dream is.

Waitress: Five tacos, one taco burger. Do you know where the American Dream is?

Lou: What's that? What is it?

Att'y: Well, we don't know, we were sent out here from San Francisco to look for the American Dream, by a magazine, to cover it.

Lou: Oh, you mean a place.

Att'y: The place called the American Dream.

Lou: Is that the old Psychiatrist's Club?

Waitress: I think so.

The scene at the taco stand is the last gasp in Duke and Gonzo's search for the American dream. They cannot define it, and it cannot be found. Perhaps the owner of Circus-Circus, the monstrous casino and club that features acrobatic and animal acts, has found *his* version of the American dream. As a child, he wanted to run away and join the circus; now he owns one.

Gonzo returns to Los Angeles, and after more ruminations on the decline of American culture, Duke muses about the media and the law enforcement establishments. The press is a "gang of cruel faggots," and journalism itself is not a profession, just a home for "fuck-offs and misfits." It is a "filthy piss-ridden little hole . . . just deep enough for a wino to curl up from the side-walk and masturbate like a chimp in a zoo-cage."[23] As for the district attorneys, they are hopeless losers, worrying about the "dangers of LSD" when it is no longer a serious threat and is used only by "drug dilletantes" such as himself.

Duke returns the battered Whale to the rental agency and takes a flight to Denver. There he pops into the airport drugstore and asks the woman be-hind the counter for amyl nitrates. That's not possible without a prescrip-tion, she tells Duke. "I'm a *doctor*," he replies, and rummages through his wallet—making certain she sees his false police badge—until he finds the card that identifies him as a "doctor of divinity." She agrees to give him the amyls. "I hope you'll forgive me, doctor," she tells him, "but I had to ask. We get some *real freaks* in this place. All kinds of dangerous addicts. You'd never believe it."[24] Duke walks out of the airport, a free man in a free country.

Tangled and Obscure Pronouncements

There are a lot of forces at work in *Fear and Loathing in Las Vegas,* and a lot of tangled and obscure pronouncements about America at the end of the 1960s. Duke and Gonzo's version of the "American Dream" is never articulated, nor is any clue provided about why they believe they will find that dream during this trip to Las Vegas. The notion seems born only of a drunken stupor at the hotel bar, when Duke draws the assignment to cover the motorcycle race and is given funds for the "free lunch, final wisdom, total coverage" undertaking.

Cast in the role of searchers, Duke and Gonzo hit the road for Las Vegas, and after several days (weeks?) limp to their separate homes, disillusioned and disappointed. But what had they expected to find? What is the "Dream," aside from the "strange torpedo" of all-expenses-paid that they choose to ride? "Buy the ticket, take the ride," Duke intones at one point,[25] and don't look back, as Bob Dylan—Thompson's muse-hero—once said.

Two chapters provide clues. These sections are not part of the chronology of the book but are instead Duke's thoughts about the nature of modern American society.

Chapter 9 is a Thompson flashback to the idyllic 1960s, as he considers his early experiences with LSD and an encounter with a Timothy Leary–like character (if not Leary himself, with his "name deleted at the insistence of the publisher's lawyer"—a common Thompson phrase). Thompson's reverie of San Francisco in that era is a charming and uncharacteristically placid scene in the book, yet it stops short of sentimentality. It is a time that Thompson obviously still regarded with great fondness when he wrote the book. Even in the midst of the gloomy days of the early 1970s, he still held some threads of the idealism of the 1960s:

There was no point in fighting—on our side or theirs. We had all the momentum; we were riding the crest of a high and beautiful wave. . . .

So now, less than five years later, you can go up on a steep hill in Las Vegas and look West, and with the right kind of eyes you can almost *see* the high-water mark—that place where the wave finally broke and rolled back.[26]

In another section, Thompson recalls at length the experience of a Colorado friend who had been traveling around the country "on sort of an early Bob Zimmerman trip." He had passed through Las Vegas, a city of decadence and high life that is supported by the excesses and sins of the nation. Because his friend was free—because he represented what they claimed to respect but what they actually feared, "freedom"—he was jailed for vagrancy and beaten. Much like the drifters in *Easy Rider,* he was shunned for being the living embodiment of what the nation was supposed to preserve and protect. So much for finding the American dream in Las Vegas.

Both these episodes serve as relatively abstract interludes in the middle of the relentless madness of the rest of the narrative, which is delivered in a brutally manic style. Sentences are short. Words come in bursts. There are fragments, joined by ellipses, delivered in machine-gun cadence. The writing attempts to keep up with the rapid-fire thought processes of a character on speed, cocaine, and LSD, and it does so rather successfully. " 'Writing' is as exact a label as the book will carry," Crawford Woods wrote in the *New York Times Book Review.* "[Its] highest art is to the drug it is writing about, whether chemical or political. To read it is to swim through the highs and lows of the smokes and fluids that shatter the mind."[27]

But what are we to make of the book's attempt at a statement, one about the "savage journey to the heart of the American Dream" promised in the subtitle? In *Fables of Fact,* John Hellmann stated that the "Dream" Thompson conceived is purely escape, and cited Thompson's rule about what to do when life becomes too complicated: "load up on heinous chemicals and then drive like a bastard from Hollywood to Las Vegas," thus making the quest into the goal.[28] At another point, Thompson turns the Horatio Alger notion on its ear. The boy who wanted to run away to join the circus had grown into a man who now owns one—Circus-Circus, the casino. For the amusement of gamblers, a gorilla is crucified (after a fashion) nightly on a neon cross that spins around in circles. The owner of Circus-Circus embodies the Horatio Alger model, in Thompson's interpretation of that story. The owner's life is the extension of that idea, as is the whole drugged escapade of Duke and Gonzo, *because someone else is paying.* That, in Thompson's view, is the embodiment of the American dream.

The reptiles Duke saw in the hotel hallucinations and in real life in the desert are in fact strong symbols of a ferocious society preying upon individuals, in Hellmann's view. There is a double irony in all of this, since Duke's hallucinations are taking place in a city that is itself a hallucination—America's dream city.

Duke and Gonzo are freaks. They act insane and abuse drugs. In Las

Vegas, they fit right in. The society is unable to recognize the sickness
within. The situation recalls Walt Kelly's Pogo: "We have met the enemy
and he is us." Thompson alternates his hallucinations with articles from the
press that reflect his horrors. As an example, one story concerns a young
man who pulled out his eyes during a drug-induced hallucination. The television newscasters bleat about the war. Gonzo exhorts Duke to turn off the
television so that they can take a drive. But the car radio plays "The Battle
Hymn of Lieutenant Calley," a right-wing apologia for the master of the My
Lai massacre. Duke does not believe what he hears and thinks it must be another hallucination. It has become impossible for him to tell the difference.

In *Fables of Fact,* Hellmann cites a scene in a desert bar as being the turning point of the book. On his return to Los Angeles after the motorcycle
race fiasco, Duke stops for a drink and talks to God. "All I did," Duke says,
"is take your gibberish *seriously* . . . and see where it got me? My primitive
Christian instincts have made me a criminal."[29] Duke draws power from this
one-sided conversation, which serves as an intermission for the two long episodes in Las Vegas. During the trip to cover the race, Duke and Gonzo
"have been moving in a state of absolute fear." Now, Duke returns to Las
Vegas to cover the drug conference and has exchanged that emotion for
loathing, and he becomes the aggressive character that he intimated he
could be.[30]

A Book of Madness and Poetry

The *New York Times* said the book contained a sense of madness that was
also poetic, and compared it favorably to such journalistic works as Norman
Mailer's *The Armies of the Night* and Tom Wolfe's *The Electric Kool-Aid
Acid Test.* The book was praised further in the *New York Times Book Review,*
which refused to make the distinction as to whether the work was fact or fiction and which called it one of the finest and truest chronicles of the 1960s
generation: "[This] is by far the best book yet written on the decade of dope
gone by. . . . [It is] a custom-crafted study of paranoia, a spew from the
1960s and—in all its hysteria, insolence, insult and rot—a desperate and
important book, . . . the funniest piece of American prose since *Naked
Lunch.*"[31]

The book was not greeted with unanimous praise. The *New Republic*
called it "more hype than book." It had important precursors. It was, the
New Republic wrote, "in the zonked, road-writing tradition of Jack
Kerouac" but lacked that writer's passion. The characters were presented in
one dimension, and there was no love in the book—no love of any kind.

The book's greatest value was in providing insights to the drug culture.[32] Other critics also questioned the book's value. Nevertheless, reviews of Thompson's subsequent work often refer to *Fear and Loathing in Las Vegas* as his seminal work, even as some sort of classic.

Hellmann cites the book as an important work because it so confounded readers as to the line between fiction and journalism. It is, in fact, Thompson's most fictionalized work, though in it he is writing about events that actually happened.

Thompson modestly considered *Fear and Loathing in Las Vegas* as a failed experiment in gonzo journalism because it was not a first draft; it was not ripped straight out of the notebook and put on the "mojo wire" (Thompson's word for telecopier) to the publisher.[33] Though the book describes a frenzy, it was the result of much craftsmanship, and that includes rewriting. Thompson called it "a fine idea that went crazy about halfway through . . . a victim of its own conceptual schizophrenia, caught & finally crippled in that vain, academic limbo between 'journalism' and 'fiction.' "[34]

Much has been said about the book as an epitaph for the 1960s, and there is that feeling of finality about it. Thompson may be making pronouncements about that decade, and if so, that factor could account for the confused and disjointed nature of the book; it has to match the times. This was the last gasp: "Because it was nice to be loose and crazy with a good credit card in a time when it was *possible* to run totally wild in Las Vegas and then get paid for writing a book about it . . . and it occurs to me that I probably just made it under the wire and the deadline. Nobody will dare to admit this kind of behavior in print if Nixon wins again in '72."[35]

It is interesting that Thompson should conclude his notes on the book with a reference to politics. Almost immediately, he was to plunge into an assignment and a year of his life that was to test the "Fear and Loathing" approach/persona against some of the traditional standards and practices of journalism: a presidential election campaign.

Chapter Six
Truth Is Never Told in Daylight

After "Fear and Loathing in Las Vegas" appeared in two *Rolling Stone* installments in the fall of 1971, Thompson was a near God to Jann Wenner. Reaction to the pieces was impressive, and Wenner wanted more from Thompson. In December of that year, the *Rolling Stone* staff met for an editorial conference at Big Sur to discuss the future of the magazine. Thompson suggested he be set up as the chief political correspondent for the magazine and turned loose on the presidential election campaign that was about to begin. Opposition from the staff was nearly unanimous. Some said politics was a turnoff, both to them and certainly to their readers, who bought *Rolling Stone* because of its focus on rock and roll. They also claimed they could not see how political reporting would fit in the magazine's format. But Thompson argued his case forcefully, and Wenner made the judgment that if Hunter S. Thompson wanted to write about presidential politics, then he would do so for *Rolling Stone*.[1]

It is interesting to note this nearly unanimous opposition to political reporting by the *Rolling Stone* staff, since within a year the magazine would be highly regarded for its coverage of the 1972 presidential campaign, and since out of that experience two books would grow that are regarded as masterpieces of modern political reporting. One, of course, was Thompson's clumsily titled *Fear and Loathing: On the Campaign Trail '72*. The other was *The Boys on the Bus*, by Timothy Crouse.[2]

Crouse's background was impressive. He had been educated at Harvard, and his father, Russel Crouse, was the coauthor of the book for Broadway's *The Sound of Music*. Yet when Timothy Crouse went to work for *Rolling Stone*, Wenner seemed to go out of his way to give him demeaning assignments. Eventually, Crouse was assigned to be Thompson's assistant during the 1972 campaign. Translated, this meant he was to keep the older reporter out of trouble. It proved, though, to be a mutually beneficial association. Thompson took Crouse seriously—as Wenner did not—and was eager to teach him how to be a reporter. He gave Crouse assignments and in one case went against Wenner's wishes and allowed Crouse to take on a major story during the Wisconsin primary. In this instance, Senator

Edmund Muskie of Maine was the expected winner of not only that spring primary but of the Democratic nomination, and Thompson was therefore at Muskie headquarters to record the victory. When the returns came in, however, Senator George McGovern of South Dakota was the surprise winner; Crouse was at McGovern headquarters, ostensibly to report on the concession speech. Wenner telephoned both his reporters long-distance and told Thompson to get over to the McGovern headquarters and take on the story. Thompson refused, since Crouse was there. But to Wenner, Crouse was "the kid" and therefore not to be trusted with a story of such significance. "The only thing you're there for is to be Hunter's legman," Wenner told Crouse. "Don't write a fucking word."³ Thompson, however, insisted, and stood over Crouse's shoulder as the young man produced an impressive story on the upset victory. It ran in its entirety in the next issue of the magazine.

Thompson was to be even more generous with Crouse. Thompson who had been shunned by the other reporters during the early days of the campaign. By the time of the Wisconsin primary, they were beginning to buddy up to him, having read his reporting in *Rolling Stone* and come to respect him. But Thompson, who could carry a grudge, decided he wanted Crouse to "do a job" on the press. Thompson had long been annoyed with the trappings of the straight press, and in no other circumstances were the shortcomings of the press more visible than during a presidential campaign. And so he told Crouse to study the reporters. "Watch those swine day and night," Thompson told him. "Every time they fuck someone who isn't their wife, every time they pick their nose, every time they have their hand up their ass, you write it down. Get all of it. Then we'll lay it all on them in October."⁴

In the two decades that followed, there was a proliferation of "media critics." A. J. Liebling of the *New Yorker* is rightfully acknowledged as the first media critic of any significance, but Crouse quickly became one of the most important pioneers of that genre with *The Boys on the Bus,* a classic that is cited and rereviewed during every presidential campaign and any other time political reporting is discussed. To a large extent, Crouse's book shows the press as a sham. In it, Crouse makes it clear that the reporters are not adversaries at all. Instead, they are an easily manipulated group that does exactly what the candidates want. The reporters travel in packs, writing essentially the same story because writing anything different would raise questions. "If this story is so great," the reporter's editor would say, "then why doesn't the *Baltimore Sun* have it?" Individualism, hard work, and initiative thus went unrewarded by the system. Blandness was esteemed.⁵ This portrayal of "pack journalism" was brutal and incisive, and it scored a direct hit on the press establishment when it was published.

Thompson, of course, was a character in the book and in some ways was its hero. He was not part of the pack. He was the iconoclast and a fulfill-ment, in a slightly twisted way, of what a reporter was supposed to be: an adversary, on the outside, dedicated to watching the caretakers and commit-ted to the purity of society. Though some reporters are presented as admira-ble, it is Thompson who is the most impressive figure. In his author's note, Crouse thanked his mentor thus: "I would like to acknowledge my debt to Hunter Thompson, who talked Jann Wenner into letting me write the *Roll-ing Stone* article from which this book grew, and who encouraged me from beginning to end."[6]

Struggles with Deadlines

Thompson's reports appeared in nearly every biweekly issue of *Rolling Stone* through the spring and summer, with a marked tapering off in the fall as McGovern's impending political massacre became apparent. The dis-patches were always the result of frenzy, again emphasizing the process of writing. As was his pattern, Thompson was at the center of his campaign coverage. The reporting and the pieces—written under deadline pressure, modified slightly, and collected in his book—show him in a constant strug-gle to get his work done, to meet deadlines, to recover from hangovers and keep the hellhounds off his trail. *Fear and Loathing: On the Campaign Trail '72* is perhaps Thompson's most significant book in terms of making an impact on the critical establishment, although the Las Vegas book is clearly much more satisfying as a work of literature.

Fear and Loathing is essentially a diary—Thompson's *Rolling Stone* arti-cles written at the time and not modified much in the process of compila-tion. He covers December 1971 until December 1972 in great detail, and the book screens that well-documented political year through his jaded sen-sibilities. At the beginning of the campaign, Thompson traveled with the members of the "straight press"—reporters from the wire services, major newspapers, and networks. These reporters at first loathed Thompson but grew to envy him. They at first resented him for his unprofessional ap-proach and attitude; they then admired him because they saw that he could write the real story of the campaign in *Rolling Stone,* whereas they had to follow the practices of conventional journalism in their reports.

The book begins with the long drive from Colorado to Washington when Thompson picks up two stoned drifters and uses them to provide an intro-duction to politics:

"We're headed for Baltimore," [Jerry] said. "What about you?"

"Washington," I said.

"What for?" Lester asked. "Why the fuck would anybody want to go *there?*"

I shrugged. We were standing in the parking lot while my Doberman pissed on the wheel of a big Hard Brothers poultry truck. "Well . . . it's a weird sort of trip," I said finally. "What happened is that I finally got a job, after twelve years. . . ."

"What *kind* of job?" Jerry asked. . . .

"It's a political gig," I said. "I'm going to Washington to cover the '72 presidential campaign for *Rolling Stone.*"

"Jesus Christ!" Jerry muttered. "That's weird! The Stone is into politics?"

I stared down at the asphalt, not sure of what to say. Was "The Stone" into politics? Or was it just *me?* I had never really wondered about it . . . but suddenly, on the outskirts of Washington, in the cold grey dawn of this truckstop near Breezewood just north of the Maryland line, it suddenly occurred to me that I couldn't really say what I *was* doing there. . . .

"It sounds like a stinking goddamn way to get back into work," said Lester. "Why don't you hang up that bullshit and we'll put something together with that car shuttle Jerry told you about?"

I shook my head. "No, I want to at least *try* this trip," I said.

Lester stared at me for a moment, then shrugged. "God damn!" he said. "What a bummer. Why would *anybody* want to get hung up in a pile of shit like Politics?"[7]

One of the characteristics of gonzo journalism is a lack of clarity about what is truth and what is fiction, and a gonzo reader must not care about the distinction too much. Did this episode happen? We don't know. It may be an internal monologue transformed into a scene with two *Rolling Stone* readers, as Thompson sweats over what he has got himself into. He is asking himself what business a rock-and-roll magazine has covering presidential politics. As Thompson said when he came into Washington in December 1971, he and his magazine were largely unknown in the nation's capital. "[N]obody had ever heard of *Rolling Stone,*" he told an interviewer. " 'Rolling what? . . . Stones? I heard them once; noisy bastards, aren't they?' It was a nightmare at first, nobody would return my calls. Washington is a horrible town, a cross between Rome, Georgia, and Toledo, Ohio—that kind of mentality."[8]

Thompson was in his comfortable role as the quintessential outsider, and obviously not part of the pack that Crouse so effectively described. He quickly learned he would find nothing of value if he followed the standard operating procedures of the political press. He learned not to do business during regular office hours, and he learned that his more effective interviews came late at night, over the telephone. As Thompson said: "In Washington, truth is never told in daylight hours or across a desk. If you catch people when they're tired or drunk or weak, you can usually get some answers. So I'd sleep days, wait till these people got their lies and treachery out of the way, let them relax, then come on full speed on the phone at two or three in the morning. You have to wear the bastards down before they'll tell you anything."[9]

Thompson's reports from the campaign were written under tremendous deadline pressure—or so he would have his readers believe. It had been a long time since he had had a job that required him regularly to file stories at such close intervals. Every two weeks he had to send his stories over the "mojo wire" to the magazine's San Francisco offices. The magazine was usually being held on the press, waiting for his article. Yet he was often in the company of reporters he admired—William Greider of the *Washington Post* and James Naughton of the *New York Times*—who had to file detailed, complex, and well-written pieces every day. To the credit of these reporters, they were sympathetic to Thompson as he suffered his biweekly breakdown.

The manic character who dominates Thompson's political dispatches cleverly obscures his shrewd style. At times, his campaign anecdotes seem to be short stories with ironic endings. The rambling, crazed style he adopts cannot, however, mask his craft. An example has to do with one of his adventures that ended up *making* news. At the beginning of the section describing this incident, Thompson learns from a news account in the *Miami Herald* that Senator Muskie's whistle-stop campaign through Florida the day before had been disrupted by activist Jerry Rubin and another man who interrupted the senator repeatedly. Rubin's companion heckled the senator viciously, making it impossible for him to speak. At one point, the man grabbed Muskie around the legs and had to be pried away. This "other man," the article reported, was wearing press credentials obtained from *Rolling Stone* correspondent Hunter Thompson.

This epigram introduces the story on an unusual note. What follows reads like a short story, yet Thompson begins at the end: with the event, the peak of the story. This item hits Thompson squarely between the eyes when he is slicing up grapefruit (with a machete, of course) for his breakfast, enjoying his late-morning hours at the Royal Biscayne Hotel in Miami. Suddenly, he finds his name in a story about a major political disturbance during the previous day's activities. He makes some calls and learns that he is being held accountable for this man's behavior, because he has apparently given his press pass to a lunatic. Like a detective who knows the murderer but needs to find the proof, Thompson knows at the beginning of the story what has happened. His job is to retrace his steps and figure out how it happened. This strategy allows the reader to learn things as Thompson learns them, and again the reporter's method *is* the story.

"Chitty and the Boohoo"

A virtue of this style is that Thompson asks the questions the reader might be asking. He questions his sources, and the reader feels like a collaborator in piecing together the facts. No example of gonzo journalism would be complete without obvious fantasy. After pulling together some of the details of the event—in which the man with Thompson's press badge wreaked havoc on the Sunshine Special, the train Muskie had chartered for a run down the Atlantic Coast—Thompson foresees a headline about a campaign train collision that killed thirty-four bystanders, the whole event blamed on a "Crazy Journalist."

After getting a reasonable account of the proceedings from his telephone source (in a conspiratorial tone he says the name "need not be repeated here"), Thompson elaborates, with accounts drawn from other stories. As he retraces his steps, he realizes where and when he has met this man who used his press credentials. The man's name is Peter Sheridan, dubbed "the Savage Boohoo" by Thompson.

A couple of nights before, Thompson had been in the company of a student journalist, Monty Chitty of the *Independent Florida Alligator* at the University of Florida. They had met Sheridan, the Boohoo, in the lobby of a Ramada Inn in West Palm Beach. The Boohoo was drunk and angry, screaming gibberish, and railing against Muskie. Normally, Thompson said, he would not have paid much attention to this sort of act, but the Boohoo had a special quality—"the Neal Cassady speed-booze-acid rap—a wild combination of menace, madness and genius." The Boohoo's behavior left Thompson with no choice but to invite him along on a ramble with Chitty. "Don't mind if I do," the Boohoo said in response to the invitation. "At this time of the night I'll fuck around with just about anybody."[10]

Thompson, Chitty, and the Boohoo end up spending about five hours together that night in West Palm Beach. Thompson offers up a few details of the Boohoo's ramble, then—in a just-between-us tone—says, "I'd like to run this story all the way out here, but it's deadline time again and the nuts & bolts people are starting to moan."[11] So he quickly wraps up the story, suggesting that the Boohoo join them on the Muskie Sunshine Special. He tells the Boohoo:

"It's the presidential express—a straight shot into Miami and all the free booze you can drink. Why not? . . . [S]ince the train is leaving in two hours, well, maybe you should borrow this little orange press ticket, just until you get aboard."

"I think you're right," he said.

"I am," I replied. "And besides, I paid $30 for the goddamn thing and all it got me was a dozen beers and the dullest day of my life."

He smiled, accepting the card. "Maybe I can put it to better use," he said.

And, of course, the Boohoo can. Thompson's closing line of the "Chitty and the Boohoo" episode is a touch worthy of the O. Henry. The structure of the piece seems at first look haphazard, at second glance clever, at third reading artful. It begins at the end and ends before the beginning. *Fear and Loathing: On the Campaign Trail '72* is rich with such pleasures, with such well-told tales.

Shut out from the traditional gatherings of the press, the "boys on the bus," Thompson had to devise his own ways of getting information any way he could. At one point, these tactics included interviewing George McGovern while standing beside him at a urinal—which gave Thompson a unique vantage point. Nor was Thompson bound by the traditions of journalism—the supposed objectivity and the practice of offering equal space to all sides of an issue.

Throughout the campaign, Thompson was a reliable source of weirdness. After the incident with the Boohoo, Thompson was banned from any of Senator Muskie's functions. But that was all right, because Muskie's fortunes were falling rather dramatically. Thompson helped seal his political doom. When the major political columnists were ruminating about what could be causing Muskie's political collapse, Thompson said—in print— that it was because he was addicted to a dangerous South American drug. Thompson said he intended the comment as a joke; nevertheless it was picked up, printed, and given authority by the straight press.

Soon after earning acceptance from the straight press, Thompson became one of its favorite characters. Reporters adopted him as a hero, but Thompson was not certain he wanted to join that particular club. Thompson's image as the leading iconoclast of the era would not allow him to become too chummy with the establishment press. He had to maintain some sort of distance and also entertain his audience. For example, a Thompson article after the convention had amused NBC anchor John Chancellor, who wrote Thompson a brief note taking him to task for an un-warranted criticism of Chancellor and NBC's performance during coverage of the Democratic National Convention. Thompson printed Chancellor's letter in its entirety, along with his reply:

Dear John . . .,
  You filthy skunk-sucking bastard! What kind of gall would prompt you to write me a letter like that sac of pus dated Aug. 11?
  . . . You dope-addled fascist bastard. I'm heading east in a few days, and I think it's time we got this evil shit cleared away. Your deal is about to go down, John. You can run, but you can't hide. See you soon. . . .
  Hunter S. Thompson.[12]

Thompson's infatuation with Senator George McGovern was visible early on. Some *Rolling Stone* editors said that Jann Wenner fancied himself as a Charles Foster Kane of the rock-and-roll generation and that Wenner wanted to deliver his readers and his generation to the feet of McGovern. Perhaps that is overstating it, but Thompson certainly put a lot of faith in McGovern and his candidacy. Although he felt a great fondness for the man, Thompson was angered by his tactics. Having earned the nomination with the "new politics" of honesty and openness, McGovern ran his campaign in the style of the "old politics." Thompson was furious, wanting to find out which member of the candidate's staff had talked him into selling out to the Democratic party establishment. As the campaign wound down and McGovern's massacre was imminent, Thompson's writing became even more caustic and bitter:[13]

This may be the year when we finally come face to face with ourselves; finally just lay back and say it—that we really are just a nation of 220 million used car salesmen with all the money we need to buy guns, and no qualms at all about killing anybody else in the world who tries to make us uncomfortable.
  . . . [W]hat a fantastic monument to all the best instincts of the human race this country might have been, if we could have kept it out of the hands of greedy little hustlers like Richard Nixon. . . .
  Jesus! Where will it end? How low do you have to stoop in this country to be president?

The long chronicle of the election campaign ends with a brief telephone conversation between Thompson and Frank Mankiewicz, McGovern's spokesman. "Keep your counsel," Mankiewicz says. "Don't draw any conclusions from anything you see or hear." Thompson then lunges into despair. "Around midnight," he writes, "when the rain stopped, I put on my special

Miami Beach nightshirt and walked several blocks down La Cienega Boulevard to the Losers' Club."[14]

A Lie-Free Report

Thompson had long been extremely critical of the straight press, and his experience in the 1972 campaign deepened his resentment of the other reporters. "Guys write down what a candidate says and report it when they know damn well he's lying," Thompson told *Newsweek*. "Half the conversation in the press bus is about who lied to whom today, but nobody ever prints the fact that they're goddamn liars."[15] Despite his occasional fabrications and stretchings of fact, Thompson prided himself on his attempt to produce the first lie-free report of a political campaign.

The *Nation's* critic was effusive in his praise of Thompson's book, calling it the most exciting work about the 1972 campaign and "one of the best books about American politics in the last decade."[16] Thompson was praised by the *Nation* for acknowledging his biases "right up front," but that sentiment was not shared by the *Columbia Journalism Review*. Thompson's argument, of course, is that "objective journalism" does not exist; the phrase is oxymoronic. He cannot offer such a bogus service, he tells us. He can only give us "honest journalism."

Attacks from the journalism establishment were inevitable. The *Columbia Journalism Review* reviled the book because its thesis was ill-founded. Wayne Booth, an English professor at the University of Chicago, reviewed the book and said it was difficult to accept the notion that Hunter Thompson was an interesting man. The book was not about presidential politics, Booth wrote, but about a middle-aged drug abuser named Hunter S. Thompson.[17] Booth's review became the party line of the journalism regulars who criticized Thompson.

Booth chose to compare Thompson's work with that of Theodore H. White, the distinguished journalist who in 1960 reinvented modern political reporting. That year White decided to cover the presidential selection process from beginning to end. It began in hotel rooms and in cluttered offices, as plans were made and strategies for primary election campaigns hatched, and it ended with the election of John F. Kennedy. White's book, *The Making of the President 1960,* was a thorough examination of the process of election. While reporting it, White was virtually alone on the campaign trail. Yet when he began researching the sequel in 1964, he found more reporters following the candidates around. By 1968, he was part of a small army. And by 1972, the press buses were packed.

For all his revolutionary work in 1960, White in 1972 represented the establishment and its staid approach to reporting. Thompson represented something else. To Booth, White was a sage, a political analyst with few peers, a mandarin of modern journalism. Thompson, on the other hand, was a punk, a braggart, an obscenity-spouting hoodlum who managed a good joke now and then. Thompson was openly hostile to politicians and was therefore unable to understand them, to interpret their motives. Thompson gave the reader very little reason to believe him. As Booth wrote, "The only reason Thompson gives us to believe what he says is what we professors of rhetoric call his ethos; he works very hard to establish his character as the main proof of what he has to say. But shit, man, his ethos ain't no fuckin' good. He again and again shows that he shares the conviction of more than a few traditional journalists that to be entertaining is more important than to tell them what happened. . . . I will believe nothing Thompson tells me, unless I have corroboration."[18]

Thompson had claimed in the introduction that he had reprinted his original dispatches as written during the heat of the campaign, so as not to tamper with the gonzo credo of "no revision." Booth decided to test this assertion by digging out old issues of *Rolling Stone* and comparing the magazine version with the book version. He found several corrections of punctuation and style, but he also found evidence that led him to believe Thompson was inserting sentences and paragraphs that would make him look more sagelike in the more permanent book than in the eminently disposable magazine. Booth suggested that perhaps these questionable sentences were in the original reports Thompson sent to the magazine but were cut out by the editors.

Booth also took Thompson to task on the question of how Richard Nixon was elected. The president appeared in Thompson's book mainly as a subject of epithet. Booth graded both White and Thompson on three points: (a) clarity and readability, (b) quality of research, and (c) analysis. White earned passing grades in all those categories, though Booth said *The Making of the President 1972* was "scarcely inspiring."[19] Thompson, on the other hand, earned three Fs. The only passing grade he earned from Booth—and it was a B-minus—was in the fourth category: "How was it on the campaign trail in 1972?" Booth credited Thompson with lashing together a reputable account of that quadrennial madness which is a presidential campaign. (White also passed, with a C.)

Booth wrote that succeeding on that one account did not make *Fear and Loathing: On the Campaign Trail '72* the masterpiece of political insight that scores of other reviewers were saying it was. Somewhere along the line, Thompson had decided that a reporter talking about himself would be more interesting than a reporter talking about events. Booth said Thompson reminded him of one of his errant students, sitting down in front of a typewriter at 2:00 A.M. with an assignment due the next morning: the student gets the idea to write about what it feels like to face that blank piece of paper. That, Booth argued, is what Thompson had done in his book. At times, the critic said, even that method failed, and Booth suspected it was just such a failure that lay behind the seventy-five-page-long transcript of the "interview" between Thompson and his editor: the writer had broken down and was unable to compose. This *Fear and Loathing in Las Vegas* trick may have slipped by Booth, but perhaps he was suggesting that a book about reality be held accountable for every little truth. Thompson could not use the same tricks he used in the Las Vegas book, because he did not claim that *Fear and Loathing in Las Vegas* was literally true.

Booth saw Thompson's book as "trivial" and did not understand the accolades that came from the finest of the journalistic breed, including David Halberstam, David Broder, and Garry Willis, who praised the book highly. As Booth wrote, "If Thompson enters future histories, it will be as an example of intellectual decline and fall."[20]

Booth's attack on gonzo journalism as a device for political reporting came at the end of a season of good reviews for *Fear and Loathing: On the Campaign Trial '72,* and the *Columbia Journalism Review* article became the subject for discussion in much of the journalistic community. Some chided Booth as if he were unable to take a joke. James Green, writing in the *Journal of Popular Culture,* said that although some of Booth's criticisms of Thompson on the grounds of taste and exaggeration had a basis, Thompson was not to be judged on the same standards as other reporters, like Theodore H. White: "[Thompson] never pretends to be a reporter—a journalist yes—but *never* a reporter. Above all else he is a writer and has never defended himself within the context of straight journalism. Nothing is sacred or off the record."[21]

Thompson answered Booth himself, the following summer in *Rolling Stone.* After one of his flights of fancy in an article on Watergate, Thompson stopped to ask himself:

What?

Do we have a libel suit on our hands?

Probably not, I think, because nobody in his right mind would take a thing like that seriously—and especially not the gang of senile hags who run the *Columbia*

Journalism Review, who have gone to considerable lengths in every issue during the past year or so to stress, very heavily, that *nothing* I say should be taken seriously.[22]

Postcampaign Political Writing

After the exhaustion of covering the campaign and pulling the book together—a task that ended in late January 1973—Thompson spent much of the rest of the year recovering and working on longer pieces for *Rolling Stone.* He was, of course, not through with politics, although his involvement would never again be as intense as it was during the 1972 campaign.

The Watergate affair and the fall of President Nixon was a reporting task Hunter Thompson would probably not have been equipped to handle. It was too traditional. It was basic police reporting: a crime had been committed and the reporters sought to take the story to its resolution. When the seriousness of the espionage at the Democratic National Headquarters became known, the *Washington Post*'s editors were faced with a tough decision. Did they allow two lower-echelon reporters to continue to cover the story? Or did they give it to some heavyweight political writers? They chose, of course, to keep Bob Woodward and Carl Bernstein on the case, and their status as outsiders in the world of political journalism allowed them to report the story more effectively than a journalist of large reputation who was "part of the club" in official Washington.

And so Woodward and Bernstein reported the Watergate story; they won a Pulitzer Prize for their newspaper; and as the scandal unfolded, the nation was put through a constitutional crisis that resulted in President Nixon's resignation. Woodward and Bernstein simply employed standard journalistic practices in their reporting, and since those practices were alien to Thompson, Watergate was not the sort of story he could effectively report. But the opportunity was too good to resist for Thompson's commentary, and in his capacity as national affairs editor for *Rolling Stone,* he "covered" the Watergate hearings.

Yet not being part of the story left a gonzo journalist impotent. Thompson's five major pieces on Watergate that appeared in 1973 and 1974 are strangely distanced from the affair. They are amusing as pieces of writing, but they do not have the manic frenzy and startlingly lucid insights of his dispatches from the campaign trail.

The first significant piece represented Thompson's emergence from the cocoon he had entered after finishing the campaign book. Utterly exhausted by the deadlines and debauchery of being a political journalist and thoroughly dismayed by the outcome of the election, Thompson had gone diving in the Gulf of Mexico, nearly drowned, got the bends, and retreated to a decompression chamber in Miami.

He presented his first extended commentary on Watergate as if it were an emissary from his longtime friend and associate Raoul Duke, now billed as the sports editor of *Rolling Stone*. He used Duke in order to exaggerate his collapse after the deadline and diving incidents of the spring of 1973, following the sheer exhaustion that came with pulling together the campaign book. In "Memo from the Sports Desk and Rude Notes from a Decompression Chamber in Miami," Duke discusses Thompson in hushed tones and speaks of his devotion to his old buddy. "Compared to the things I've done for Thompson," Duke says, "both Gordon Liddy and Howard Hunt were stone *punks*."[23] Allegedly concerned for Thompson's health, Duke insists that he be allowed time for full recovery in order to shake the traumas of the previous eighteen months. But the Watergate coverage will no doubt lure him to Washington, Duke fears, with serious consequences for Thompson's health.

Thompson uses Raoul Duke to mythologize his own character and personality, giving himself a larger-than-life status that will be one of the constants of the Watergate pieces. He portrays himself as being in a death struggle with Richard Nixon, "his old football buddy."[24] (Thompson and Nixon had, in fact, shared a limousine ride in 1968, during which they had a long and detailed discussion about the National Football League. Nixon's knowledge of the game impressed Thompson, who pronounced the president a "stone fanatic" on the subject.)[25] Nixon had been a focus of Thompson's writing for five years, and Thompson here puts himself on a level with the president, to make the Watergate crisis look like a death struggle between the two. Nothing will keep Thompson away from Washington. He wants to watch the destruction of the man he calls "a walking embarrassment to the human race,"[26] a man "whose entire political career has been a monument to the same kind of cheap shots and treachery he finally got nailed for."[27]

The Duke/Thompson piece was a device merely to announce Thompson's return to the scene after a six-month absence. He was back on the case at the *Rolling Stone* National Affairs Suite in Washington. Now, the article implied, Nixon's days were numbered. The tremendous ego evident in this piece was uncharacteristic of most of Thompson's gonzo journalism. Although always focused on Thompson, most gonzo articles were self-deprecating and he rarely portrayed himself in an entirely positive light. But fresh from the two "Fear and Loathing" successes, the Thompson in the

"Rude Notes from a Decompression Chamber" seems self-conscious and hyper-aware of the image he now must maintain.

The first full story on the scandal, "Fear and Loathing at the Watergate: Mr. Nixon Has Cashed His Check," shows Thompson in a rare generous mood toward the straight press. After initially bungling the story, Thompson was now willing to say that it had become "probably the most thoroughly and most professionally covered story in the history of American journalism."[28] He needed to be generous. Watergate was not his story; he was riding on the coattails of the press establishment he had for so long mocked. He did not really *cover* the story; he *watched* the story, usually on television. He could not stand to be in the hearing room and report on it. All he could do was comment, and that distance from the action renders the Watergate pieces enjoyable but not—as his campaign reporting had been—incisive. Thrust into this armchair role, Thompson was able to vent his alternating rage (at White House arrogance and gall) and delight (at the impending fall of the empire). Beyond that, there was nothing for him to do:

I was seriously jolted, when I arrived in Washington, to find that the bastards [the press] had this Watergate story nailed up and bleeding from every extremity— from "Watergate" and all its twisted details, to ITT, the Vesco case, Nixon's lies about the financing for his San Clemente beach-mansion, and even the long-dormant "Agnew Scandal."

There was not a hell of a lot of room for a Gonzo journalist to operate in that high-tuned atmosphere.[29]

As it turned out, Thompson had been in the Watergate complex the night of the burglary, drinking in the hotel bar and discussing pro football with one of his buddies. But that is as close as he comes to being part of the story. Much of "Fear and Loathing at the Watergate" and the next piece in the series, "Fear and Loathing in Washington: The Boys in the Bag," is devoted to a series of conversations between Thompson and his compadres, condemnations of the antics of President Nixon and his staff, and glee at the justice Thompson is certain will be done. At times, these articles break down into true gonzo, with long sections devoted to his notes, written in telegraphic phrases and presented with generous ellipses, ampersands, abbreviations, and other symbols of manic writing. Thompson had discovered, after a few attempts at covering the Senate Watergate hearings themselves, that the hearing room was precisely the wrong place to be. He spent most of his time, then, "covering" the hearings from a Capitol Hill bar and, eventu-

ally, retreating to his home in Woody Creek, Colorado, to watch the proceedings. The more he watched—the more he learned about the Nixon
White House—the more bile rose in Thompson's throat. It was like a journey into the heart of darkness and Thompson in fact evokes Conrad directly
at the end of one piece, with the phrase "Mistah Nixon, he dead."[30]

The *Rolling Stone* articles allowed Thompson to ramble. Wenner gave
Thompson whatever space he needed to tell his story, and the self-
indulgence of these pieces allowed them to run to phenomenal lengths.
When Thompson wrote a brief New Year's Day piece for the *New York
Times*, he had no such luxury, and his writing was therefore tighter and,
since it was for a more general audience, a bit more mannered. Yet "Fear and
Loathing in the Bunker," as the *Times* piece was called, was just as biting as
any of the *Rolling Stone* articles, with its parallels between Richard Nixon
and Adolf Hitler. Though Thompson was obviously enjoying Nixon's
downfall, he did not see much joy in the future:

One of the strangest things about these five downhill years of the Nixon Presidency
is that despite all the savage excesses committed by the people he chose to run the
country, no real opposition or realistic alternative to Richard Nixon's cheap and
mean-hearted view of the American Dream has ever been developed. It is almost as
if that sour 1968 election rang down the curtain on career politicians.

This is the horror of American politics today—not that Richard Nixon and his
fixers have been crippled, convicted, indicted, disgraced and even jailed—but that
the only available alternatives are not much better; the same dim collection of
burned-out hacks who have been fouling our air with their gibberish for the last
twenty years.[31].

There was no joy in Mudville when the game was over. Thompson's last
Watergate piece, "Fear and Loathing in Limbo: The Scum Also Rises," was
filled with sputtering rage, as Thompson reacts to President Ford's pardoning of Nixon, which denies the nation the right to see the man imprisoned.
Nixon, "that rotten, sadistic little thief," had got away again.[32] This long
epitaph for the Nixon presidency does have a moment when Thompson and
Nixon come face to face . . . . or nearly so. On the day after Nixon's resignation speech, Vice-President and Mrs. Ford are escorting President and Mrs.
Nixon to the helicopter that will take them to the airport, where they will
board *Air Force One* for the flight to California. While in midflight, Ford
will be sworn in as president. Thompson is standing with other members of
the press, near the helicopter. Nixon is walking across the White House
lawn "like a wooden Indian full of thorazine"[33] when he finds himself look-

ing at Hunter Thompson, wearing official White House press credentials: "His face was a greasy death mask. I stepped back out of his way and nodded hello, but he didn't seem to recognize me. I lit a cigarette and watched him climb the steps to the door of the helicopter. . . . Then he spun around very suddenly and threw his arms straight up in the famous twin-victory signal; his eyes were still glazed, but he seemed to be looking over the heads of the crowd, at the White House."[34]

Nixon left, and after Thompson's postmortem, the journalist too said good-bye to politics. It was as if without Nixon to "kick around" anymore, the political game would not be fun for Hunter Thompson. He turned to other games.

Chapter Seven
This Sporting Life

After politics, Thompson's major obsession has been sports. The parallels between the two are obvious, and the one often employs the vernacular of the other. Covering the 1972 presidential campaign "was like watching pro football teams toward the end of a season," Thompson said. "Some of them are coming apart and others are picking up steam; their timing is getting sharper, their third-down plays are working. They are just starting to peak."[1] Thompson, who bet compulsively on pro football, also bet on politics. Even Watergate could be discussed in sports terminology:

Nixon . . . talked about politics and diplomacy in terms of power slants, end sweeps, mousetrap blocks. Thinking in football terms may be the best way to understand what finally happened with the whole Watergate thing: Coach Nixon's team is fourth and 32 on their own ten, and he finds out that his punter is a junkie. . . . When the game ends in disaster for the home team, then the fans rush onto the field and beat the players to death with rocks, beer bottles, pieces of wooden seats. The coach makes a desperate dash for the safety of the locker room, but three hit men hired by heavy gamblers nail him before he gets there.[2]

After covering the campaign and writing about Watergate for two years, Thompson was ready to walk off the political field and into new arenas. Some of his first writing had been done as a stringer at high school football games, and that early experience in sportswriting under pressure had an effect on his work. The manic intensity demanded by the tight deadlines following late-night games helped define the style later known as gonzo.

Sportswriting was thus a natural home port after Thompson's years of exile as a political reporter. There was even some continuity to it all, as he considered his shared limousine ride with Richard Nixon on the campaign trail in 1968. "That was the only time in 20 years of listening to the treacherous lying bastard that I knew he wasn't lying," Thompson remembered.[3] As Nixon wished aloud that he could start all over in his career and exchange politics for sportswriting, Thompson just smiled. "The scene was so unreal," Thompson recalled, "that I felt like laughing out loud—to find myself zipping along a New England freeway in a big yellow car, being chauffeured around by a detective while I relaxed in the back seat and talked about football with my old buddy Dick Nixon, the man who came within 100,000 votes of causing me to flee the country in 1960."[4]

Pro football was Thompson's shared obsession with Nixon, and his writings about that sport, as well as about boxing, are bizarre but nonetheless lucid examples of those sportswriting genres. Thompson's writing about fishing is perhaps his best writing about sports.

Of course, as with politics, sports was just an *excuse* to Thompson, a framework for his commentaries about society. "The Kentucky Derby Is Decadent and Depraved" had used the horse race as a launching pad for a long blast at conservative society. The race itself had consumed barely more than a paragraph of the article. Such was often the case with his stories about sport.

Football and Politics

Fear and Loathing: On the Campaign Trail '72 ended with a scene at the Super Bowl. Thompson built on that sketch the following year in the much-longer "Fear and Loathing at the Super Bowl."[5] This article is similar to his coverage of the presidential campaign, in that it turns into an attack on sportswriters who follow athletes around, much like the "boys on the bus" who trail candidates obediently. But in the world of professional sports, there is the additional element of team owners, league executives, and others that Thompson would classify as vermin.

The 1974 Super Bowl in Houston pitted the Minnesota Vikings against the Miami Dolphins. This was the era of the immovable, unstoppable Dolphins, led by quarterback Bob Greise and offensive stars Mercury Morris, Jim Kiick, and Larry Csonka. Yet the game would be a mere backdrop to the real action: the mob of "drunken sports writers, hard-eyed hookers, wandering geeks and hustlers (of almost every persuasion), and a legion of big and small gamblers."[6] Thompson presents himself as a doctor of divinity (not as a doctor of gonzo journalism, as he had occasionally in the past) and ministers to his congregation in the Hyatt Regency in Houston, from the twentieth-floor balcony in the huge atrium of the hotel. His shouted sermon came just before dawn and drew heavily from the Book of Revelation. After the events of the previous two years, Thompson said, his sermon was inevitable. He would explode if he did not make the "crazed and futile effort to somehow explain the extremely twisted nature of my relationship with God, Nixon and the National Football League," which had "long since become inseparable" in his mind.[7] And yet Thompson does not offer many clues to what he actually said in his sermon, beyond his need to publicly embarrass Al Davis, owner of the Oakland Raiders, and to confess his chagrin at discovering that he actually agreed with Richard Nixon about something—professional football.

As with the political writing, Thompson's story on the Super Bowl concerned itself with process, with his struggle to write the article. "Fear and Loathing at the Super Bowl" is perhaps one of his best examples of metajournalism. The deadline, which so often vexes him, is given living form in the story, appearing as a leech. Sweating, hung over, held captive in his hotel room by the madness outside the door in Super Bowl–week Houston, he feels a movement at the base of his spine. He begins clawing at his back and discovers a leech—"huge, maybe eight or nine pounds." Now it becomes a race: can Thompson finish the article before the leech sucks all the blood from his body? He writes, "[A]s a professional sportswriter I knew that if the bugger ever reached my medulla I was done for."[8] The presence of the leech inspires him to make his dawn sermon on the balcony, alternating shouts of "hallelujah!" and "four more years!" Then he begins to unleash the article in a frenzy.

Much of what he writes is an attack on the sporting press ("hired geeks," he called them in *Fear and Loathing in Las Vegas*). The sportswriters descending on Houston for the Super Bowl are supposed to be the best American journalism has to offer, but they are stupid ("there are only a handful of sportswriters in this country with enough sense to pour piss out of their own boots," Thompson declares)[9] and gullible (with a straight face, Thompson tells a fellow scribe that he had spent Super Bowl–week in a seven-dollars-a-night motel in Galveston shooting heroin; the guy believes him).

Thompson's original conception of the piece was to follow one team through the last months of the season as it prepared for the Super Bowl and along the way to document the Nixonian similarities between pro football and politics. Accordingly, he attached himself to the Oakland Raiders, though that team ended up not making it to the Super Bowl. Nonetheless, Thompson's investigation led him to other interesting areas—the hypocrisy of the team owners and the issue of drugs in professional sports. At his first practice, Thompson realizes that the "strange-looking bugger named 'Al,' who looked like a pimp," was Al Davis, general manager and owner of the Raiders. The fact that Al Davis was a millionaire while former Hell's Angel Sonny Barger was in jail was a sign, to Thompson, that American society was sick.[10] Davis had Thompson booted from practice because he heard that the reporter was a "drug fiend" and might corrupt the football players.

The irony, of course, is now obvious, some two decades later, after drug scandals in professional sports have filled the sports sections with monotonous regularity. Every aspect of the game is riddled with drug abuse. Thompson recalls betting heavily with "wealthy cocaine addicts"[11] and associating with sportswriters who were under the influence of alcohol and other drugs as they looked down on a stadium full of raving drunks. Why *shouldn't* the players be high, he reasons. Everyone else is. The players recognize the irony. As one Pittsburgh Steelers lineman tells Thompson during a discussion about drug testing, if there was a halftime urine test conducted in the press box, the writers would protest vociferously. Yet the players might be subject to such tests.

Thompson has always professed affection for sports. Indeed, as one visitor to his Colorado home said, "[I]n the Thompson household, only first-strike and avalanche have priority over basketball and football games."[12] Thompson enjoys playing the games himself and has some gifts as an athlete. One writer remarked on his physical condition, considering that his reputation is that of a serious drug abuser: "[H]e looks like an off-duty split end for the Miami Dolphins."[13]

It is the commercialization and bastardization of sport that infuriates and at times disillusions Thompson. From the mid-1960s to the mid-1970s, he said, he had seen a change in professional football. It had been a "very private kind of vice," and going to the game was a great way to unwind with a lot of kindred spirits. But all that changed: prices doubled, the crowd mutated from blue-collar to white-collar, and the game itself became big business, a multimillion-dollar enterprise. Thompson blames television for a good deal of these changes.

The Super Bowl was precisely the kind of manufactured spectacle that television devoured. Yet it was nothing but an elaborate decoration, sort of an "emperor's new clothes." Two two-week preface to the Super Bowl and particularly the seven days before the game, were nothing but hype—hype fed on by the media and perpetuated by the media. "Almost anything would have been better than the useless week I spent in Houston waiting for the Big Game," Thompson writes.[14] The NFL's big party two days before the game, called the Incredible Texas Hoedown, "was as wild, glamorous and exciting as an Elks Club picnic on Tuesday in Salina, Kansas."[15]

Thompson summons the memory of legendary Green Bay Packers coach Vince Lombardi, known for his credo, "Winning isn't everything. It's the only thing." That was not an accurate summary of Lombardi's feelings,

Thompson tells us. Lombardi was not interested in winning but simply was interested in not losing. His credo was to avoid mistakes and to hope one's opponent made them. Lombardi's approach was effective. It worked so well, Thompson writes, that Richard Nixon, a close friend of Lombardi's, adopted it. Don Shula, the head coach of the Miami Dolphins, also used the Lombardi approach, and that was why his team was, in Thompson's estimation, one of the dullest teams in the history of pro football. It was a well-oiled machine, all precision, but no fire, personality, style, or wit—much like the rest of American society in 1974. The Super Bowl trophy is named after Vince Lombardi, and Thompson describes it as having "all the style and grace of an ice floe in the North Atlantic"[16] and as representing what has been lost in the game and in society.

"Voodoo, Black Magic and Witchcraft"

One of Thompson's first major failures involved coverage of the world heavyweight championship fight between George Foreman and Muhammad Ali later that year in Kinshasa, Zaire. It was to be Thompson's most troublesome assignment. He claimed to have been unnerved by the African experience because there was "too much voodoo, black magic and witchcraft."[17] Thompson ended up contracting malaria, missing the fight, and writing not a single word about it.

George Plimpton did write about the fight. Plimpton, author and editor of the *Paris Review*, had performed a highly successful experiment in participatory journalism when writing about his tenure as a last-string quarterback for the Detroit Lions in summer camp. The book, *Paper Lion*,[18] was a huge success and legitimized the first-person point of view as a form for the New Journalists—the form Thompson had used so successfully. Plimpton met Thompson on the flight to Africa, and they became friends, Plimpton eventually chronicling Thompson's time in Zaire in his book about prizefighting, *Shadow Box*.[19] The book's cover was a painting of Archie Moore, Muhammad Ali, Norman Mailer, Ernest Hemingway, George Plimpton, and Hunter Thompson, all sitting around a locker room and wearing monogrammed sweat suits.

Thompson appears to have had great fun in Kinshasa; at least, his concern with voodoo is never portrayed in Plimpton's book. Instead, he signs his checks "Martin Bormann" and seems obsessed with the notion that Nazi criminals are hiding in the Congo forest; he suggests that Plimpton join him in a mission to do a low flyby and roust Bormann out. These concerns distract Thompson, and Plimpton reports that he never showed up at the press conferences or sparring sessions, leaving those small concerns for the traditional sportswriters. This arrangement was fine with Thompson's readership, or so Plimpton reasoned. Those readers were "not interested in the event at all—whether it was the Super Bowl, or politics, or a championship fight in Zaire—but only in how the event affected their author. So, in fact, the only reporting Thompson had to do was about himself."[20] Plimpton uses Thompson well in the book, as if he were a fictional creation. He is a delightful, somewhat oafish bumpkin, as Plimpton describes him: "a big, loose-limbed figure wearing a pair of dark aviator sunglasses, a purple and strawberry Acapulco shirt, blue jeans, and a pair of Chuck Taylor All-Star basketball sneakers that seemed too large for his feet."[21]

Plimpton eventually loses track of Thompson but finds him several days later:

I asked him about the fight.

"What fight? Oh, I didn't go to the fight. I stayed in my hotel swimming pool. I lay on my back and stared at the moon coming up and the only person in the hotel came and stared at me a long time before he went away. Maybe he thought I was a corpse. I floated there naked. I'd thrown a pound and a half of marijuana into the pool—it was what I have left and I am not trying to smuggle it out of this country—and it stuck together there in sort of a clot, and then it began to spread out in a green slick. It was very luxurious floating naked in that stuff, though it's not the best way to obtain a high."

"No," I said.

"But a very luxurious feeling nonetheless."

Although many of Thompson's admirers were disappointed to learn that he would not be reporting on Muhammad Ali's unbelievable comeback in Zaire, Thompson was able to produce a piece about Ali's third—and successful—attempt to regain the heavyweight championship, in a match with Leon Spinks in 1978.

The story brought Thompson to familiar turf, with its own weird style of "voodoo, black magic and witchcraft": the city of Las Vegas. Thompson's "Last Tango in Vegas" appeared in two parts, and they are so different from each other as to have been written by two individuals. The first part, subtitled "Fear and Loathing in the Near Room," is as close as Thompson has ever come to writing a traditional magazine feature. He is not at the fore of this piece very often. In a style more reminiscent of Tom Wolfe's, it focuses on the characters around Muhammad Ali: the bodyguards, the armies of assistants, the hangers-on. Similar in structure to a classic magazine profile, it has bites of the style and madness of Tom Wolfe's best work.

Ali's world is, to Thompson, "an orbit so high, a circuit so fast and strong with a rarefied air so thin that only 'The Champ,' 'The Greatest,' and a few close friends have unlimited breathing rights."[22] Thompson uses this opportunity to offer a benediction on Ali's career as he retires in greatness, having reclaimed his crown three times, a feat unparalleled in boxing. But his achievements went beyond the ring; he was greater than his chosen sport. And when he was defeated by Spinks in their first match, "a whole generation went over the hump as the last Great Prince of the Sixties went out in a blizzard of pain."[23] Much of white America cheered, Thompson writes, because "that uppity nigger from Louisville had finally got what was coming to him. For fifteen long years he had mocked everything they all thought they stood for: changing his name, dodging the draft, beating the best they could hurl at him. . . . But now, thank God, they were seeing him finally go down."[24]

Ali was, in Thompson's view, one of the few real martyrs "of that goddamn wretched war in Vietnam" and a hero everywhere in the world but in his own country. "No Viet Cong ever called me 'nigger,' " Ali told the press when he announced that he would not comply with his induction orders. Stripped of his heavyweight title in the 1960s, he was reinstated in the early 1970s after a long battle, and had made two remarkable comebacks in the boxing ring. After losing the decision in the Spinks fight, Ali's announcement that he would rule the boxing world again was greeted with groans.

The first installment of "Last Tango in Vegas" is amusing, yet strangely distant and not at all characteristic of Thompson's writing. It ends, however, with a cliff-hanger. Thompson describes a prank being played on Ali, and Ali, in turn, playing a joke on one of his associates. Midway through the anecdote, the article ends. In the next issue of *Rolling Stone,* part 2—subtitled "Fear and Loathing in the Far Room"—has Thompson returning to center stage, and again the main issue is his struggle to *get the story.* Harold Conrad, one of Ali's employees, has promised Thompson a seat next to the Champ on a flight to New York. Ali claims to know nothing of this deal and shoos Thompson away. In New York, Thompson vents his rage at Conrad and is promised a private audience with Ali.

He gets it. Thompson is invited into Ali's room, where the Champ is in bed, seminude, with his wife and several associates. Thompson first commits a transgression that no one else has been allowed to do: smoke in the Champ's presence. He then begins spouting obscenities, which Ali does not like his wife to hear. Nevertheless, Ali gives Thompson a lot of leeway, and the writer holds court, sitting cross-legged on the dresser, greatly amusing the Champ and his contingent. Eventually, Thompson runs off to his room, gets a zip-on Satan mask, and returns to Ali's suite, where he prances around, shouting weird slogans. Ali is at first frightened, then delighted. He borrows the mask and uses it to scare one of his bodyguards.

The ice broken, Ali gives Thompson a long, detailed, and lucid interview on the art and science of boxing and his plans for the Spinks fight in Las Vegas. Thompson notes that George Plimpton, Norman Mailer, Budd Schulberg, and most of the other major writers of his generation who professed to love the sport skipped the second Ali-Spinks fight, perhaps wishing to avoid seeing the destruction of the greatest fighter of the century. Plimpton had quoted Hemingway's advice—not to get too close to a boxer, because it would be tragic to see him destroyed. But Thompson was there to record Muhammad Ali's final victory.

"Last Tango in Vegas" is a near deification of Muhammad Ali, and one of the few times when Thompson is effusive in praise of a human being. Although the Champ was perhaps the most famous man on the planet (at least, the most recognized one), he remained a mysterious figure. Millions of words have been written about him, but few offer insight into his character or break down the layers of defenses. Thompson realizes that his words cannot knock down the defenses either. He had learned an essential lesson about fame, and had learned that all the accolades did not prevent Ali from remaining a mystery, a "brown Jay Gatsby" who had "an endless fascination with that green light at the end of the pier."[25] Ali became the Crown Prince of the World. "He came, he saw, and if he didn't entirely conquer," Thompson wrote, "he came as close as anybody we are likely to see in the lifetime of this doomed generation."[26]

"Last Tango in Vegas" was an unusual and schizophrenic piece of writing for Thompson. The first half was well mannered, restrained, and mainstream in its approach, like something an ambitious New Journalist would write. It has few traces of gonzo. The second part was more in Thompson's usual metajournalism style, yet filled with uncharacteristic admiration for his source. It also contained a resignation letter of sorts, in which he says the piece is "my final adventure in fish-wrap journalism and I frankly don't give a fuck if it makes any sense to the readers."[27] "Last Tango" became, in fact, one of Thompson's last pieces for *Rolling Stone*.

Adventure on the High Seas

Sailing and fishing are two sports in the adventure-writing tradition that would seem to be natural subjects for Hunter S. Thompson. But his first major voyage into this area was not successful. Assigned by *Scanlan's* to cover the America's Cup yacht race in 1970, he never published a story drawn from that experience, although Ralph Steadman, a collaborator on the piece, eventually published his drawings.[28] Thompson and Steadman had met in New York and got on the flight to Newport, Rhode Island, together; on the flight, they took some pills Thompson had in his possession. His goal was to be as "unhinged" as possible. He was successful in that pursuit, as he and Steadman attempted some serious vandalism in the course of their reporting. Under cover of night, they rowed out to the Australian challenger, armed with spray paint, planning to write "Fuck the Pope" on the side.[29] Fortunately for the Australians, they were diverted from their task.

Many of Thompson's adventures have taken place at sea, and once, while sailing from Bermuda to Aruba, he was mistaken for a winner of the America's Cup.[30] After the aborted America's Cup assignment, his next story on the high seas was to bear more journalistic fruit.

Playboy assigned Thompson to cover a fishing tournament near Cozumel, Mexico, and the result was one of his funnier adventures, "The Great Shark Hunt."[31] As with his work on politics, football, and boxing, the subject takes a backseat to whatever concerns of the moment occupy Thompson. "The Great Shark Hunt" is a bit like *Fear and Loathing in Las Vegas* in its conception as Thompson and a companion—Yail Bloor, in this case—are handed a prime assignment, all expenses paid, for "free lunch, final wisdom, total coverage." Yet here Thompson is greeted with courtesy by the resort's employees, as some sort of hero in his role as a "genuwine, real-life '*Playboy* writer.' "[32] The hotel staff call him "Señor Playboy," and he is encouraged to make use of all facilities and to charge everything to either the magazine or the boat manufacturer sponsoring the junket.

He makes a serious attempt at coverage of the event, but the story turns into a rollicking account of his adventures with Bloor, as they remain one step ahead of the authorities. They are, of course, using drugs, because these provide a welcome alternative to their real assignment. "I'm damned," Thompson writes, "if I can remember anything as insanely fucking dull as that Third Annual International Cozumel Fishing Tournament."[33]

In subject matter, "The Great Shark Hunt" is reminiscent of some of Ernest Hemingway's journalism about sport. Hemingway's fishing stories, such as "On the Blue Water"[34] and "The Great Blue River,"[35] often use the adventure as a backdrop for commentaries on society and for sermons on the nature of courage and diatribes on writing. In "Monologue to the Maestro: A High Seas Letter,"[36] Hemingway takes on a college student as a deckhand. Dubbed the Maestro (for his skill with the violin, sometimes shortened to

"Mice"), he proved to be not much of a sailor. Mice, of course, wants to be a writer and has therefore attached himself to Hemingway. Hemingway tells him, "You certainly must be going to be a hell of a good writer because you certainly aren't worth a damn at anything else."[37] Holding forth with the Maestro, the boards of the ship's deck creaking as the waves lap against the bow, Hemingway reluctantly talks about writing for the Maestro's benefit: "Good writing is true writing. If a man is making a story up it will be true in proportion to the amount of knowledge of life that he has and how conscientious he is; so that when he makes something up it is as it would truly be. If he doesn't know how many people work in their minds and actions his luck may save him for a while, or he may write fantasy. But if he continues to write about what he does not know about he will find himself faking. After he fakes a few times, he cannot write honestly anymore."[38]

Perhaps the Maestro did not exist; perhaps he was a composite of a score of young men who pursued Hemingway as if he were some guru of writing. Whatever the case, there are similarities between Hemingway's "chatty letters" from his home in Cuba and Thompson's writing from a similar locale. Like Hemingway, Thompson uses being out on the water merely as excuse to offer a variety of opinions, and the subject—again, as with Hemingway—occasionally includes writing:

I'd spent a week on this goddamn wretched story and I still didn't have the flimsiest notion of what deep-sea fishing *felt like*. I had no idea what it was like to actually catch a big fish. All I'd seen was a gang of frantic red-neck businessmen occasionally hauling dark shadows up to the side of various boats, just close enough to where some dollar-an-hour mate could cut the leader and score a point for "the angler. . . ."
  [I]t was this half-crazed sense of frustration that led me finally to start wandering around the docks and trying to find somebody to take me and Bloor out at night to fish for man-eating sharks. It seemed like the only way to get a real feel for this sport—to fish (or hunt) for something genuinely dangerous, a beast that would tear your leg off in an instant if you made the slightest mistake.[39]

The actual shark hunt is a small part of the adventure. Thompson and Bloor secure a boat, a small shark is caught, and it is brought aboard to flop on deck for a while and then to be shot four times in the head. "Hemingway had the right idea," Thompson writes, "when he decided that a .45-caliber submachine gun was the proper tool for shark fishing." But Thompson suggests aiming the barrel at another prey. "Why shoot the innocent fish," he asks, "when the guilty walk free along the docks, renting boats for $140 a day to drunken dupes who call themselves 'sport fishermen'?"[40]

The real adventure comes not aboard the fishing boat but when Thompson and Bloor try to leave the country. On the plane, they realize that they have a lot of drugs on them and will be unable to go through customs at San Antonio. Thus, they eat every drug they have in their possession, and barely escape without being caught. "[M]y feeling for national politics," Thompson writes, "is about the same as my feeling for deep-sea fishing."[41]

The Curse of Lono

Thompson took to the high seas again in 1983 for *The Curse of Lono,*[42] perhaps his most underrated work. It came after a long period of relative dormancy for Thompson, and a full decade after the frenzy of covering the campaign. The story is told without the high speed of his political reporting, and he allows something akin to sentimentality to creep into his writing. There is a real sense of awe in the book, and an appreciation of the beauty of nature, as Thompson and Steadman go to Hawaii for another in their series of adventures.

Retained by *Running* magazine to cover the Honolulu Marathon, Thompson lures his illustrator to the islands with an exotic scheme about how, without any training whatsoever, they can win the race. What follows is a generally hilarious account of their time in Hawaii, in which the race, of course, is of little concern. Most of the attention is paid to consuming alcohol, carousing, and going deep-sea fishing. Thompson uses a character named Gene Skinner, whom readers logically assume is a real human being. As Thompson has admitted in print, however, Skinner is fictional. Raoul Duke has retired, thanks to cartoonist Garry Trudeau, who appropriated the name to use with Thompson's likeness in "Doonesbury." Skinner is to serve the same purpose as Duke, but with a different attitude. The Skinner alter ego is not as nice as Duke, Thompson has said. "It is a brutal attitude," he told a critic, "anti-humanist. What I'm trying to do is create a character to fit the times. It's a whole new style."[43] There does not appear to be much new about the style, except that the writing has more of a "revised" feel than anything since the publication of *Fear and Loathing in Las Vegas. The Curse of Lono* came after a long layoff, and shows more polish and maturity.

When Thompson lands in Hawaii, he is met at the airport by Skinner, who smiles and says, "I thought you quit this business." Thompson responds, "I did, but I got bored."[44] A number of long conversations between Thompson and Skinner hint at schizophrenia, as Thompson's internal monologues debate issues and strategies. Steadman serves the role of companion/confidant, a role he has played before (as have Oscar Acosta,

Bill Cardoso, and others). Steadman is a good foil for Thompson's outrageousness, and the two serve as a literary comedy team.

Thompson intersperses his writing with Mark Twain's notes on Hawaii and with generous excerpts from the journals of William Ellis, who traveled to the islands in the mid-1850s, and Richard Hough, who wrote *The Last Voyage of Captain Cook*.[45] Thompson uses these excerpts to introduce the story of Captain James Cook, who had come to Hawaii in the late 1700s and been mistaken by the natives for the Hawaiian god Lono; when they discovered their error, the natives killed Captain Cook. Thompson begins to imagine that he is now Lono, perhaps feeling that he is not what he is supposed to be. At times, Thompson seems lost amid the world of deep-sea fishing and drugs, yet continues, somehow, to live the way he has for most of his journalistic career: on an expense account. The metajournalism theme reappears in *The Curse of Lono*, as might be expected.

Thompson's fondness for Ralph Steadman is one of the central motifs of the book, some of which is written in the form of letters to his friend. He invites Steadman on the assignment, but a back injury forces the illustrator to return to London. Thompson pelts him with letters. The most exciting sections about fishing come in these letters. For example, Thompson Steadman about the marlin he caught, "a beast the size of a donkey that is fighting for its life on its own turf. A ten-pound trout might put up an elegant fight, but a 300-pound marlin with a hook in its throat can rip your arm-bones right out of their sockets, then leap right in the boat and snap your spine like a toothpick. The marlin is a very mean fish and if it ever develops a taste for human flesh we will all be in trouble."[46]

Returning to shore after his battle with the marlin ("Old Gonzo and the Sea"), Thompson is suddenly possessed with the notion of what the Western culture has done to the Hawaiian Islands. Bellowing from atop the ship's mast, he creates such a commotion that a huge crowd is attracted—horrified—to where his boat is tying up. One spectator says it sounded like "the second coming of Lono." That is all the evidence Thompson needs. "That's me, Ralph," he writes his friend. "I am the one they have been waiting for all these years. Captain Cook was just another drunken sailor who got lucky in the South Seas."[47] Trying to lure Steadman back to Hawaii, Thompson turns to the mystic:

So don't worry about me, Ralph. . . . But I would naturally appreciate a visit, and perhaps a bit of money for the odd expense here and there.

It's a queer life, for sure, but right now it's all I have. Last night, around midnight,

I heard somebody scratching on the thatch and then a female voice whispered, "You knew it would be like this."

"That's right!" I shouted. "I love you!"

There was no reply. Only the sound of this vast and bottomless sea, which talks to me every night, and makes me smile in my sleep.[48]

The Curse of Lono was not greeted with overwhelming praise by critics. Most said it would be acceptable to fans of Thompson's previous work but was unlikely to enlarge his audience. Indeed, it may have baffled his admirers with its headfirst dive into Hawaiian lore. Yet the mystical last section of the book was a rare psychic journey into parts of Thompson's brain that he had not previously held up for examination. To some critics, *The Curse of Lono* was nearly self-parody. The *New York Times Book Review* said that if *Fear and Loathing in Las Vegas* had been an experiment, as Thompson claimed it had, then *The Curse of Lono* was the control, as he put his more or less "real self" through the motions of gonzo journalism.[49]

Thompson's experience in Hawaii had affected him deeply, and he picked up his discarded novel from the 1960s, *The Rum Diary*. Although *Fear and Loathing in Las Vegas* and *The Curse of Lono* were fictionalized to some extent, the novel would be his first extended experiment with fiction. The book concerned pirates and was in some ways an outgrowth of the *Lono* experiment. But it was discarded again, and Thompson was pulled into journalism's nets once more. He said he was a journalist because "I would not be anything else, if for no other reason than I'd rather drink with journalists. Another reason I got into journalism: you don't have to get up in the morning. . . . Imagine hanging out with lawyers. Now everybody wants to be a lawyer or a banker."

Despite his supposedly large intake of drugs and alcohol and his near-death experiences on the road, Thompson had survived long enough so that by age fifty he could qualify for curmudgeon status and emerge as a serious social critic for the last decade of the twentieth century.

Chapter Eight

The Gonzo Papers

There was a sudden and marked falling off of Thompson's output after he left *Rolling Stone*'s Washington bureau in the mid-1970s. Concentrating on an annual article for *Rolling Stone*, he retracted his hatred of all politicians long enough to give Jimmy Carter a ringing endorsement. He mourned the disappearance of Oscar Zeta Acosta (Dr. Gonzo from *Fear and Loathing in Las Vegas*) in the magazine's tenth-anniversary issue, he covered the sensational Roxanne Pulitzer divorce trial in Palm Beach, and he wrote stories on other major events of American popular culture.

He published much less, and his writing was sometimes criticized as being an imitation of his earlier days of glory. Yet Thompson remained popular; issues of *Rolling Stone* with his stories sold better than those without; he still commanded a healthy speaker's fee for his tour of campuses; he was an icon of the era. Actor Bill Murray portrayed him in *Where the Buffalo Roam*. Pulitzer Prize–winning artist Garry Trudeau used him as the model for "Uncle Duke" in his "Doonesbury" comic strip.

Rolling Stone editor Jann Wenner missed Thompson's regular contributions to the magazine. Wenner had given the journalist a lot of freedom and Thompson had run with it, bringing *Rolling Stone* a great deal of acclaim for its coverage of popular culture. Wenner fretted over Thompson's relative silence. The magazine had spent a substantial amount of money to send Thompson to cover the Ali-Foreman fight in Zaire but had no story to show for it.

Part of the reason Thompson's output for the magazine slowed stemmed from a simmering feud he had with Wenner over money. The editor had gone to Colorado and got his star reporter to agree to cover the 1976 presidential campaign and to prepare another book manuscript. The working title was *Fear and Loathing: On the Campaign Trail '76*. Editor and author saw no reason the past could not be repeated. Thompson took the seventy-five-thousand-dollar advance Wenner offered. Then, not long after returning to San Francisco, Wenner sold Straight Arrow Books, the *Rolling Stone* subsidiary that was to publish the new book. Thompson was furious and would not accept Wenner's calls for months. But in the spring of 1975, while Thompson was watching a remarkable film from Southeast Asia on the television news, Wenner called to ask, "How would you like to go to Saigon?"[1] Thompson could not pass up what he thought might be the perfect assignment.

It turned out to be something less than perfect. Although Thompson was able to maintain his life-style—he hired a couple of Vietnamese boys to walk behind him carrying a cooler full of beer—the experience was not the sort of thing he usually enjoyed writing about. Thompson was frightened in Saigon, victimized by street thugs, and certain the world would end at any moment. He braced himself for that end with large doses of amphetamines and beer. This medicine had an effect on him. Traveling into the bush with two reporters, Thompson sighted incoming helicopters landing in a clearing and insisted they were giant locusts. As the two reporters interviewed the South Vietnamese soldiers disembarking from the helicopters, Thompson took a walk, stumbling within a hundred yards of a Vietcong encampment. Back in Saigon, he was nearly killed in a street shooting. Wenner cabled Thompson that he was no longer on retainer. Thompson was furious and said that he was there, in Saigon, on Wenner's "greed-crazed instructions," that there was a "very high personal risk factor," and that there should be "big green on the barrelhead for anyone who stays."[2] Wenner's reply was his attempt to wash his hands of the incident: he said if Thompson wanted to leave Saigon, he should. And although Thompson wanted to be there for the fall, the North Vietnamese had issued a number of warnings that journalists would not be recognized as noncombatants. Thompson was stubborn, though, and asked for the help of the U.S. Marines when the time came to evacuate. Two days before the fall, he escaped to Laos and, eventually, to Colorado.[3]

Wenner ran only two pages of Thompson's eventual article in *Rolling Stone,* disappointing the fans who expected the definitive gonzo article to come out of a war zone. A decade later, Wenner published the complete article. Just why he withheld the piece for so long is baffling; perhaps his relationship with Thompson was so strained that it affected his editorial judgment.

Thompson published only two articles in *Rolling Stone* in 1976 and 1977. The first was a political contribution, "Fear and Loathing on the Campaign Trail '76: Third-Rate Romance, Low-Rent Rendezvous."[4] In this piece, Thompson discovers, to his disgust, chagrin, and everlasting consternation, that he has met a politician he actually *likes,* a man he believes can be trusted. It is one of Thompson's most personal statements, and he is a writer known for personal statements. It is also a characteristically astute and brutal political analysis and, at the same time, a naive testament to hope and justice. The piece opens with samples, drawn from the newspapers, of the world's weirdness (an elderly man in Fort Lauderdale throwing bowling balls into the sea because he thinks they are "nigger eggs"; an organized ring of dog castrators loose in the Miami suburbs), followed by the bizarre announcement that Hubert Humphrey considered himself a viable candidate for the presidency. Humphrey had received a great deal of Thompson's wrath in the 1972 book (in which Thompson had suggested Humphrey be castrated to ensure there could be no more of his kind); now Thompson fears that Humphrey, or at least the Old Politics he represents, will triumph in 1976. The story is too depressing to cover, Thompson writes, and he does not plan the "free lunch, final wisdom, total coverage" gig this time: "I will leave the dreary task of chronicling this low-rent trip to Teddy White, who is already trapped in a place where I don't want to be."[5] (He makes no mention of the aborted book contract that would have trapped him in that place, along with White.)

Thompson's hatred for politicians is a recurring theme in his work. He despises Humphrey, despises Scoop Jackson, despises Richard Nixon, "who was criminally insane and also president of the United States."[6] But something happened to Thompson in 1974 that he is still reeling from in 1976. In 1974, Thompson was traveling with Senator Edward Kennedy and accompanied the senator to the University of Georgia, where Kennedy was to speak at the law school. The governor of the state spoke first, and Thompson was overwhelmed by the power of the speech. Here was Governor Jimmy Carter, addressing a group of the state's wealthiest lawyers and attacking them as representatives of a system that rewarded dishonesty. It was a brave speech to make, in Thompson's opinion, and afterward he asked the governor for a copy of the text. There is no text, Carter told him; he was speaking extemporaneously. Thompson managed to get a copy of a cassette recording that had been made, and he carried it around for two years, playing it to anyone who would listen and sometimes just listening to it alone, to remind himself that there was hope. When "Jimmy Carter and the Great Leap of Faith" was published in *Rolling Stone,* Thompson insisted that the tape be transcribed and the Law Day speech be run in its entirety with the article.

Wenner angered Thompson with the cover line used to advertise this very personal statement of finding faith in the sinful world of politics: a beatific portrait of Carter smiled out to *Rolling Stone* readers, the cover line reading, "An Endorsement, with Fear and Loathing, by Hunter S. Thompson."[7] Thompson liked Carter but did not want that liking perverted into an endorsement of anybody. The editor-writer relationship was further strained.

The Banshee Screams

To celebrate the magazine's tenth anniversary the following year, Wenner planned a special issue and sought a major contribution from his most famous writer. Wenner expected something lucid, insightful, and earthshaking, perhaps on "the meaning of the 1960s," that might lure readers. Instead he got another extremely personal piece from Thompson, this time devoted to his missing friend Oscar Zeta Acosta.

Thompson had last seen Acosta five years before, and "The Banshee Screams for Buffalo Meat"[8] was his attempt to trace what had happened to his friend. Acosta, the unconventional attorney Thompson had profiled in "Strange Rumblings in Aztlan," had served as the model for Dr. Gonzo in *Fear and Loathing in Las Vegas*. And though Random House had accepted that book for publication, its lawyers advised against releasing it, even if it was classified as a novel. The character of "Dr. Gonzo" was clearly Acosta, as any careful reader of Thompson's work could tell. Thompson's manuscript told about many violations of the law that Acosta had committed. He could sue for libel, the lawyers argued. He could be disbarred.

Thompson agreed to track down Acosta and get him to sign a consent form. As the book was awaiting its 1972 publication, Acosta's reaction baffled the Random House attorneys: the only thing he objected to was being called "Samoan." Thompson refused to change that reference, but Acosta insisted that the dust-jacket copy identify him as the inspiration for Dr. Gonzo.

Acosta had apparently been involved in drug running, and in his article Thompson pulled together as many stories as he could about the attorney's experiences and speculated on his whereabouts. Thompson later admitted that one of the purposes of "The Banshee Screams for Buffalo Meat" was to be so provocative as to draw Acosta's interest. He intended seriously to libel Acosta, just to see if he would respond. When Acosta did not, Thompson was certain that his friend was dead.[9]

The Acosta article was not the sort of thing one would have expected Thompson to contribute to the all-star anniversary issue marking *Rolling Stone*'s first decade (a two-hour network television show accompanied the issue). Yet "The Banshee Screams" piqued the attention of filmmakers, and a project based on the story eventually made it to theaters three years later, under the title *Where the Buffalo Roam*. Thompson served as a consultant on the film and provided a voice-over narration. It was a wretched film, but it did feature a shatteringly accurate portrayal of Thompson by former "Saturday Night Live" star Bill Murray. Peter Boyle portrayed the Acosta ("Oscar") role, and he provided slapstick amusement. But the deep sensitivity and hurt that Thompson had shown in his strange epitaph for his friend were lost amid the heavy-handed comedy in the film. For a film devoted to a man who claimed to be fiercely devoted to the large truths in life, it was a film that represented large fictions.

The Great Shark Hunt

Thompson's 602-page retrospective, *The Great Shark Hunt,* subtitled "Gonzo Papers, Vol. 1," appeared in 1979. It was a crazy quilt of a book, with no apparent order to its contents. No editor's notes illuminated the circumstances under which the pieces were written. They were just thrown together into four sections—the first a collection of seminal gonzo pieces, the second Thompson's political writings, the third his *National Observer* and "straighter" articles, and the fourth a few of his more recent pieces, the three or four articles he had written in the preceding five years.

Because it offered no explanation about his career, no analysis of his work, not even a time line or a chronology, the book was not a good introduction to Hunter Thompson, and such an introduction might be needed. Thompson had not, after all, published much for the previous half-decade. First-time Thompson readers could easily find themselves perplexed by the bulky volume.

In his brief author's note, written well over a year before publication, Thompson describes himself sitting in his publisher's office the night before Christmas Eve, contemplating leaping out the window to the fountain many floors below. But he changes his mind. As he wrote, "I probably won't do it (for all the wrong reasons), and I'll probably finish this table of contents and go home for Christmas and then have to live for 100 more years with all this goddamn gibberish I'm lashing together."[10] Thompson later said he was suicidal as he sat on the crest of forty, with his marriage crumbling beneath him.[11]

This weighty book brought together many pieces previously unavailable, save in deteriorating copies of *Scanlan's*. "The Kentucky Derby Is Decadent and Depraved" remained an outstanding achievement, and "The Temptations of Jean-Claude Killy" was still venomously funny. In addition to the newspaper and magazine pieces, extensive selections from the three books were also included.

The Great Shark Hunt was generally greeted with much acclaim and afforded critics the opportunity to assess the first twenty years of published Thompson writing. In the *New Republic,* critic William Plummer noted Thompson's courage at attacking "moving targets" in his political writing. H. L. Mencken had mercilessly ridiculed William Jennings Bryan during the 1925 Scopes trial in Tennessee, and did not pause to eulogize movingly after Bryan's death.[12] Like Mencken, Thompson was an unrelenting critic of politicos who, in Plummer's words, "managed to be both plain-speaking and unscrupulous, somehow at the same time. Plus he was wickedly funny, unless, of course, you were Ed Muskie and minded it being 'reported' in *Rolling Stone* that you were taking an exotic form of South American speed throughout the campaign."[13]

One of the most flattering reviews came from an unusual source: conservative columnist William F. Buckley, Jr. Buckley said that Thompson elicits "the same admiration one would feel for a streaker at Queen Victoria's funeral."[14] In the *Nation,* critic Gene Lyons wrote that Thompson "knows more about Americans and the national condition than many of his sterner and more responsible colleagues in the press."[15]

Tightening the Screws

Thompson was again withdrawn for much of the 1980s. His only major publication of the early part of the decade was *The Curse of Lono,* which earned mixed reviews and mild sales. He made one last trip for *Rolling Stone,* covering the sensational Roxanne Pulitzer divorce trial,[16] in which he tried to alter his writing to reflect the attitude of the 1980s. "I'm starting to tighten the screws a little now," he said. "No more Mr. Nice Guy. . . . It is a brutal attitude, anti-humanist."[17] Indeed, Thompson's sexist characterization of Ms. Pulitzer was as offensive or "brutal" as one could want:

She was an incorrigible coke slut, [Pete Pulitzer] said, and a totally unfit mother. She stayed up all night at discos and slept openly with her dope pusher, among others. There was a house painter, a real estate agent, a race car driver and a French baker— and on top of all that, she was a lesbian, or at least some kind of pansexual troilist. In six and a half years of marriage, she had humped almost everything she could get her hands on. . . .

[Watching her in court, Thompson muses:] Roxanne Pulitzer is not a beautiful woman. There is nothing especially striking about her body or facial bone structure, and at age thirty-one, she looks more like a jaded senior stewardess from Pan Am than an international sex symbol. Ten years on the Palm Beach Express have taken their toll, and she would have to do more than just sweat off ten pounds to compete for naked space in the men's magazines.[18]

Thompson's only other *Rolling Stone* publication in the 1980s was the decade-old "Dance of the Doomed,"[19] published in its entirety. Thompson's account of the fall of Saigon is perhaps one of the purest examples of what he hoped gonzo journalism would be. It has the feeling of having been assembled, rather than written. It is a scrapbook made up of many things: verbatim transcriptions of interviews; cables exchanged between Wenner and Thompson; snatches of relevant song lyrics; a scene from Graham Greene's *The Quiet American;* clippings from newspapers; and brief, vivid excerpts from Thompson's journals. There does not appear to be any revision. In a cable to Wenner, Thompson reports stalking the street with a Vietnamese teenager, carrying an M-1 and looking for danger, but "all we saw worth shooting was a gaggle of huge rats."[20]

For a writer often known for making himself the center of the story, Thompson did not often allow readers to glimpse the personal, dark recesses of his soul. The true horror of Vietnam, however, seemed to have had a blistering effect on him. His journal passages are like stolen looks into an intimate, private diary:

For a while it looked like we were going to be blown right out of here. And that is no exaggeration. It appeared that we would leave by helicopter if we were lucky. And most of us would be unlucky and suddenly dead. But all of a sudden it's changed. The zip is gone. There's no sense of danger. Nothing pushing. There's just a flatness that was very evident tonight at the table [of journalists] in the garden. The same group, but the level of humor was not up to par at all. I'm tired but not that tired.

Now there's fighting in goddamn Laos. There's no end to it. No end.[21]

The fall of Saigon was the perfect story for the gonzo treatment. It has the power and vision of some of the better accounts of the Vietnam War, including Michael Herr's hypnotic *Dispatches.*[22] Delayed in publication for ten years, "Dance of the Doomed" made a fitting epitaph for Thompson's association with *Rolling Stone.* It was the best example of gonzo since the *Fear and Loathing* books and was an appropriate closing piece to bring down the curtain on that part of his career.

Working for Hearst

In 1985 *San Francisco Examiner* editor David Burgin talked his boss, publisher William Randolph Hearst III, into hiring Hunter Thompson as an *Examiner* columnist. The idea seemed insane, from both sides of the issue. Thompson was known for erratic behavior; could he *produce* the column a week that the *Examiner* wanted? He did not appear to be able to produce much of anything anymore, his output had dwindled so. And from Thompson's side, there was the question of going to work for a Hearst. As Thompson once said, Hearst newspapers are "a monument to everything cheap, corrupt and vicious in the realm of journalistic possibility."[23] Yet the Hearst-Thompson marriage was made, Thompson met his weekly deadlines, and he even became the first *Examiner* columnist to become syndicated since the days of Hearst the elder, grandfather to Will Hearst.

Will Hearst aggressively marketed his newspaper and cajoled Thompson into appearing in a television advertisement for it. In the ad Thompson is shown at a shooting gallery, when Hearst approaches and asks him to become the media critic for the *Examiner.* Thompson continues firing, then says, "Why not? We will chase them like rats across the tundra."[24] The final frame of the commercial shows Thompson's target, with an obliterated bull's-eye.

The *Examiner* columns at first focused on whatever interested Thompson and then began to zero in on the media in the late 1980s. It was the closest thing Thompson had done to "real journalism" in a long time, yet his reportorial abilities were still in order. He predicted the resignation of Supreme Court Chief Justice Warren Burger a day before his surprise announcement.[25]

Thompson's columns also managed to maintain some of his characteristic energy and frenzy within the strict space limitations (approximately seven hundred words) and the confines of writing for a broader audience than he had in *Rolling Stone.* The *Examiner* was a family newspaper, which meant the copious drug references and obscenities had to be left out. Some critics found it difficult to imagine gonzo without those elements, but Thompson's style was so distinctive and provocative that it could survive without some of these more obvious flourishes.

In 1988, Thompson collected several of his columns in his second retrospective, subtitled "Gonzo Papers, Vol. 2." *Generation of Swine* was an indictment of a society that had been molded by the Ronald Reagan sensibility. Reagan had emerged, like a soft-spoken, imbecilic Nixon, as Thompson's new muse. Of the cast of Republican characters, Thompson wrote,

Nixon was genetically criminal. Agnew was born wrong. Ford was so utterly corrupt that he made millions by pardoning Nixon, and Reagan is beginning to take on the distinctly Spanish physical characteristics of the Somoza family, formerly of Nicaragua.

When this one [the Iran-Contra scandal] finally unravels, it will make Watergate look like a teen-age prank, and Richard Nixon will seem like just another small-time politician who got wiggy on greed and cheap gin.[26]

Reagan and Bush had poisoned the country, in Thompson's view, and given birth to a "generation of swine." Doing research at a mall supermarket-theater after a showing of *Rocky IV,* Thompson studied the audience emerging from the Commie-baiting Stallone film. There they were, with "[h]uge brains, small necks, weak muscles and fat wallets—these are the dominant physical characteristics."[27] The climate seemed perfect for commentary by Hunter Thompson: there were "new politicians to gore, new pomposities to puncture."[28] Pulled together, these columns paint an ugly portrait of an era, and Thompson shows himself to be a man out of his time, desperately trying to make sense out of that which has no sense. Whether he is writing about politics, other social issues, or events in popular culture, Thompson presents himself as central to the story (as we would expect), and yet as someone who does not belong.

He frequently quotes himself in these pieces ("We were somewhere on the freeway near the San Diego Zoo"[29] is reminiscent of the opening of *Fear and Loathing in Las Vegas*), also quotes the Book of Revelation ("I love the wild power of the language and the purity of the madness that governs it," he writes),[30] and falls back on the Hemingway influence that has always been strong in his work (the closing line "Then I walked back to the hotel in the rain"[31] is a dead lifting of the end of *A Farewell to Arms*).

The pressure of the weekly deadline forced Thompson to produce, and most of that output is good. Although he had flirted again with writing a novel, in *Generation of Swine* he seems to have realized that nonfiction is his art. Journalism in whatever form it took when it came out of Hunter Thompson was a seductive force, despite its many disadvantages: "I have spent half my life trying to get away from journalism, but I am still mired in it—a low trade and a habit worse than heroin, a strange seedy world full of misfits and drunkards and failures. A group photo of the top ten journalists in America on any given day would be a monument to human ugliness. It is not a trade that attracts a lot of *slick* people; none of the Calvin Klein crowd or international jet set types. The sun will set in a blazing sky to the east of Casablanca before a journalist appears on the cover of *People* magazine."[32]

This work was met, again, with a mixed critical reception. Herbert Mitgang, writing in the *New York Times,* noted that Thompson's pieces "combine name-calling, bomb-throwing and sardonic humor." "He's a little more strident this time out," Mitgang wrote, "but if you happen to share his public enemies, Mr. Thompson's your man."[33] Trying to put this unique style of nonfiction writing in perspective, Mitgang calls upon the specters of William Randolph Hearst and Joseph Pulitzer, and their sensationalistic style called yellow journalism. But even that parallel does not do justice to Thompson. "Nearly everything he writes makes yellow journalism pale," Mitgang wrote.[34]

Political writer Curtis Wilkie of the *Boston Globe* gave *Generation of Swine* high praise. He said Thompson's political writing "has regained the intensity of his work in *Rolling Stone* magazine nearly 20 years ago. . . . He is back in command of his career."[35]

Generation of Swine actually made the best-seller lists, reestablishing its author as a commercial force in modern nonfiction. He retained his position as *Examiner* columnist and continued to meet the obligations and responsibilities of a working journalist, despite the predictions of those critics who had suggested he could not keep up the output for more than a couple of months. More *Examiner* columns were collected in *Songs of the Doomed* in 1990, which also featured Thompson's reflections on four decades of life as a journalist.

If Thompson at fifty was no longer writing the revolutionary prose of twenty years before, his writing and the writing of many of his contemporaries reflected his breakthroughs with gonzo journalism. If gonzo as a style of writing *could* mature, then it had done so with *Generation of Swine* and *Songs of the Doomed.*

Chapter Nine

"When the Going Gets Weird, the Weird Turn Pro"

Hunter S. Thompson's life has unfortunately garnered much more attention than his art. He has thrust himself actively into his work, so that no matter what he begins writing about, he ends up writing about Hunter S. Thompson. He has created an unusual image of himself—that of a drugged, burned-out psychotic whose sensibilities allow the horrors of society to resonate within his charged soul.

It is an interesting image for him to have. He is southern, "raised a God-fearing, well-mannered little Kentucky gentleman."[1] He has a compassionate and sensitive side, but it is not often portrayed in his work or in articles about him. He is described as "wise, ethical, and extremely vulnerable to other peoples' opinions," and this "seems more the myth than the myth itself, so methodically has it been stowed away."[2] His family maintains that he does not encourage the public perception of the wild and crazy journalist. His brother James said, "Hunter is not comfortable with his image, but it is carved in stone."[3] The writer is, of course, responsible to some extent for watering and manuring the public "character" of Hunter Thompson. He sanctioned the film *Where the Buffalo Roam,* in which "Hunter Thompson" says, "I don't advocate the use of weird chemicals and violence, but they worked for me."[4] Such tactics do not make it appear as if Thompson is trying very hard to dispel his image. In fact, his legend has made him a lot of money and it therefore rules him. His motto, ascribed to Raoul Duke, is "When the going gets weird, the weird turn pro." He has made a profession out of weirdness.

Thompson often blames cartoonist Garry Trudeau for perpetuating the wilder aspects of the gonzo character, through "Uncle Duke" in "that fucking 'Doonesbury,'" as Thompson calls Trudeau's hugely popular syndicated comic strip. Of Trudeau, Thompson has said, "Never met him, never even seen him . . . he's too small to see. . . . I feel sorry for his parents. They worked and sacrificed to put him through Yale, and all he learned was to live like a leech."[5] Once, Trudeau suggested that the Duke character was a womanizer. Thompson wrote him to suggest that he drop that story line or face death.[6] "People think it's a joke," Thompson told an interviewer, "like I get paid for it or something. You know, me and Garry must be big buddies. Well, fuck that. . . . All this stuff avoids coming to the point that matters, which is what I turn out. Funny, I almost never get questioned about writing."[7]

His image is of concern here because it often threatens to overshadow his work. It is the image that casts doubt upon his credibility in the minds of some critics. Journalism of any kind—even gonzo journalism—must be accurate in all its particulars, some critics argue. Thompson answers with a chorus of raspberries; he is in business to find some larger truth, something beyond the journalist's litany of who, what, where, when, why, and how.

From the beginning, Thompson's style divided critics. Most admired the "stunt" behind *Hell's Angels* and savored the details in his reporting. Yet as he further immersed himself in his writing, so as to blur the lines between fact and fiction, the critics divided. *Fear and Loathing in Las Vegas* was acceptable, because it could easily be read as fiction. But *Fear and Loathing: On the Campaign Trail '72* angered much of the traditional journalistic community. Though some critics called it one of the best pieces of writing on politics, others made the valid point that it really is not about politics. Although Senator George McGovern is praised, we learn nothing about him. There are no insights to his character. There is no attempt whatever to try to understand Richard Nixon's psyche.

Many writers appear to have influenced Thompson, and two are worth particular mention. A comparison to H. L. Mencken is appropriate. Both are master stylists. Reading Mencken today, we realize how little we learn about the events he supposedly covered. The same comment can be made about Thompson. His style of attack is another point on which he can be compared with Mencken. Mencken's assaults on the mountebanks of his day are not dissimilar from Thompson's mad-dog tirades. Hemingway is another obvious influence, in theme and style. Hemingway's spare prose appears to have made an impact on Thompson as he sat in his cubbyhole at *Time* magazine, retyping his work. In Thompson's writing, there are frequent references to drugs; Hemingway's drug was whiskey.

Not all critics would be pleased with these comparisons which place Thompson with such august company. Journalist Joseph Nocera wrote that his rereading of Thompson's early work was embarrassing.[8] "The writing seemed pedestrian, the points tortured," Nocera wrote. "What I found embarrassing, of course, was that I had been such a hard-core fan."[9] Thompson is merely a relic and is guilty of repetition, in Nocera's view: "Can it really be that the work of someone so universally praised such a short time ago can seem so thin and insubstantial today?"[10] While reading Thompson, Nocera remembered his own college days, and noted that the writer routinely referred to police officers as "pigs," the fashion of the times. Indeed, other critics assailed Thompson on his use of stock characters, charging that "stereotyped characters are prime targets for his 'Gonzo' journalism."[11]

New Journalism and particularly gonzo journalism are subversive in intent. The persistent message, one scholar wrote, is that "we are all a tad loony."[12] That is an accurate characterization of the anarchy described in Thompson's writing. That was a symptom of the era. He benefited from being in the right place in the right era and having a clever idea. He is short on understanding and long on stereotyping in the *Fear and Loathing* books, but an argument can also be made that as a journalist, he is merely reporting what he sees.

Thompson appears to have modified his style in recent years, perhaps in some attempt to reflect the times. The "no more Mr. Nice Guy" approach he employed for "A Dog Took My Place" is an example of the vindictive, self-righteous style he deems suitable for the era of Ronald Reagan and George Bush. The toned-down escapades of *Generation of Swine* show that Thompson's work can be forceful without the copious references to drugs and alcohol that dominated his writing two decades ago.

The New Journalism debate has been raging for nearly thirty years, and it will continue. Some critics argue that it is a bastard form, that there is no way to marry journalism with the techniques of fiction. Others make a strong case for the New Journalists as historians of the present. As the form is attacked, praised, debated, and reviled, one likely point of agreement would be that none of those writers who pioneered the genre has done so much with such bizarre energy as Hunter S. Thompson. Whether it is mere fashion or journalism with value, Thompson's writing will remain an important chronicle of the era. His stories are, he puts it, "strange tales from a strange time."

When he was approaching fifty, Thompson told *Boston Globe* reporter Curtis Wilkie that "it only feels like one long year since I was twenty-two. I never grew up."[13] Yet his thoughts occasionally turn to mortality. In a hotel room in Zaire, George Plimpton asked Thompson what his "death fantasy" would be. Thompson replied:

Well, vehicular, of course—something in a very fine car. Back in the U.S., there was a mountain I used to drive over in the sixties on the way down from Louisville past

Birmingham to the Eglin Air Force Base—Iron Mountain, I guess they call it: a lot of big houses upon it and rich people from Birmingham and the road is sort of scenic, with big entranceways and fine views, and there's one place where you come around a sharp curve to the left, and straight ahead, down beyond the cliff, is the city, acres of steel mills and Bessemer furnaces and smelting yards below—and my concept of death for a long time was to come down that mountain road at a hundred and twenty and just keep going straight right there, burst out through the barrier and hang out above all that . . . and there I'd be, sitting in the front seat, stark naked, with a case of whiskey next to me, and a case of dynamite in the trunk . . . honking the horn, and the lights on, and just sit there in space for an instant, a human bomb, and fall down into that mess of steel mills. It'd be a tremendous goddamn explosion. No pain. No one would get hurt. I'm pretty sure, unless they've changed the highway, that launching place is still there. As soon as I get home, I ought to take the drive and just check it out.[14]

Appendix

Interview, March 1990

William McKeen: Your North American articles for the *National Observer* in 1963 seem so much more sedate than your dispatches from South America in 1962 and early 1963. Were there some problems in dealing with the *Observer* when you were closer to the editors?

Hunter S. Thompson: When I came back from South America to the *National Observer,* I came as a man who'd been a star—off the plane, all the editors met me and treated me as such. There I was—wild drunk in fatigues and a Panama hat. I said I wouldn't work in Washington. *National Observer* is a Dow Jones company so I continued to write good stories—just without political context. I drifted West. *National Observer* became my road gig out of San Francisco. I was too much for them. I would wander in on off hours drunk and obviously on drugs asking for my messages. Essentially, they were working for me. They liked me, but I was the bull in the china shop—the more I wrote about politics the more they realized who they had on their hands. They knew I wouldn't change and neither would they.

Berkeley, Hell's Angels, Kesey, blacks, hippies . . . I had these *connections*. Rock and roll. I was a crossroads for everything, and they weren't making use of it. I was withdrawn from my news position and began writing book reviews—mainly for money. The final blow was the Wolfe review. I left to write *Hell's Angels* in 1965.

WM: What was the nature of the conflict with the *Observer* over the coverage of the Free Speech Movement at Berkeley?

HST: The Free Speech Movement was virtually nonexistent at the time, but I saw it coming. There was a great rumbling—you could feel it everywhere. It was wild, but Dow Jones was just too far away. I wanted to cover the Free Speech Movement, but they didn't want me to.

My final reason for leaving was because I wrote this strongly positive review of Wolfe's *Kandy-Kolored Tangerine Flake Streamline Baby*. The feature editor killed it because of a grudge. I took the *Observer*'s letter and a copy of the review with a brutal letter about it all to Wolfe. I then copied that letter and sent it to the *Observer*. I had told Wolfe that the review had been killed for bitchy, personal reasons.

WM: You spent some of your time at Time, Inc., typing the works of Faulkner, Fitzgerald, and other great writers in an effort to understand their style. What writers have had the greatest influence on you?

HST: I would type things. I'm very much into rhythm—writing in a musical sense. I like gibberish, if it sings. Every author is different—short sentences, long, no commas, many commas. It helps a lot to understand what you're doing. You're writing, and so were they. It won't fit often—that is, *your* hands don't want to do *their* words—but you're *learning*. Writers of greatest influence? Conrad, Hemingway, Twain, Faulkner, Fitzgerald ... Mailer, Kerouac in the political sense—they were allies. Dos Passos, Henry Miller, Isak Dinesen, Edmund Wilson, Thomas Jefferson.

WM: Did writing sports have an effect on your writing that writing news might not have had? I'm curious, because some of the best American writers (Lardner, Hemingway, even Updike) covered sports in one way or another.

HST: Huge. Look at the action verbs and the freedom to make up words—as a sports editor, you'll have twenty-two headlines and not that many appropriate words. At the Air Force base, I'd have my section: flogs, bashes, edges, nips, whips—after a while you run out of available words. You really get those action verbs flowing.

I put it all together once with my farewell to sports writing, but I always come back to it under odd circumstances: Ali, the Kentucky Derby, even the Mint 400.

WM: What caused the rift with *Rolling Stone?* Was it something that was building for a while, or was it directly related to the "Great Leap of Faith" article?

HST: Wenner folded Straight Arrow Books shortly before the Saigon piece. I had to write that piece because the war had been such a player in my life for ten years. I needed to see the end of it and be a part of it somehow. Wenner folded Straight Arrow at a time when they owed me $75,000. I was enraged to find that out. It had been an advance for *Shark Hunt.* I wrote a seriously vicious letter—finally saying all I was thinking as I was taking off for Saigon. While in Saigon, I found I'd been fired when Wenner flew into a rage upon receiving the letter. Getting fired didn't mean much to me. I was in Saigon, I was writing—except that I lost health insurance. Here I was in a war zone, and no health insurance.

So, essentially, I refused to write anything once I found out. I found out when I tried to use my Telex card and it was refused. I called *Rolling Stone* to find out why (*perfect* phone system right to the end of the war). I talked to [managing editor] Paul Scanlon, who was sitting in for Wenner (off skiing). He told me I was fired, but fixed my telex card, etc. The business department had ignored the memo to fire me because it'd happened too many times before. They didn't want to be bothered with the paperwork, so Wenner's attempt had been derailed.

Anyone who would fire a correspondent on his way to disaster. . . . I vowed not to work for them. It was the end of our working relationship except for special circumstances. About that time, they moved to New York. *Rolling Stone* began to be run by the advertising and business departments and not by the editorial department. It was a financial leap forward for Wenner and *Rolling Stone,* but the editorial department lost any real importance.

You shouldn't work for someone who would fire you en route to a war zone.

I got off the plane greeted by a huge sign that said, "Anyone caught with more than $100 U.S. currency will go immediately to prison." Imagine how I felt with $30,000 taped to my body. I was a pigeon to carry the *Newsweek* payroll and communication to those in Saigon. I thought we'd all be executed. It was total curfew when we got off the plane so we were herded into this small room with all these men holding machine guns. There I was with three hundred times the maximum money allowance. We got out and I leapt on a motor scooter and told the kid to run like hell. I told Loren I wouldn't give him the money until he got me a suite in a hotel. Not an easy task, but he came through.

"The Leap of Faith:" I had already picked up on Carter in '74. It was a special assignment as everything was after Saigon. I was still on the masthead: it was an honor roll of journalists, but the people on it—well, all of them were no longer with *Rolling Stone.* I didn't like that they put on the cover that I *endorsed* Carter. I picked him as a gambler. Endorsing isn't something a journalist should do.

Essentially, the fun factor had gone out of *Rolling Stone.* It was an outlaw magazine in California. In New York it became an establishment magazine and I have never worked well with people like that.

Today at *Rolling Stone* there are rows and rows of white cubicles, each with its own computer. That's how I began to hate computers. They represented all that was wrong with *Rolling Stone.* It became like an insurance office with people communicating cubicle to cubicle.

But my relationship had ended with the firing. The *attempt* was enough.

WM: Your use of drugs is one of the more controversial things about you and your writing. Do you think the use of drugs has been exaggerated by the media? How have drugs affected your perception of the world and/or your writing? Does the media portrayal of you as a "crazy" amuse, inflame, or bore you?

HST: Obviously, my drug use is exaggerated or I would be long since dead. I've already outlived the most brutal abuser of our time—Neal Cassady. Me and William Burroughs are the only other ones left. We're the only unrepentant public dope fiends around, and he's seventy years old and claiming to be clean. But he hasn't turned on drugs, like [Timothy] Leary.

As for my perception of the world and my writing, drugs usually enhance or strengthen my perceptions and reactions, for good or ill. They've given me the resilience to withstand repeated shocks to my innocence gland. The brutal reality of politics alone would probably be intolerable without drugs. They've given me the strength to deal with those shocking realities guaranteed to shatter *anyone's* beliefs in the higher idealistic shibboleths of our time and the "American Century." Anyone who covers his beat for twenty years, and that beat is "The Death of the American Dream," needs every goddamned crutch he can find.

Besides, I *enjoy* drugs. The only trouble they've given me is the people who try to keep me from using them. *Res ipsa loquitur.* I was, after all, a literary lion last year.

The media perception of me has always been pretty broad. As broad as the media itself. As a journalist, I somehow managed to break most of the rules and still succeed. It's a hard thing for most of today's journeyman journalists to understand, but only because they can't do it. The smart ones understood immediately. The best people in journalism I've never had any quarrel with. I *am* a journalist and I've never met, as a group, any tribe I'd rather be a part of or that are more fun to be with—in spite of the various punks and sycophants of the press. I'm proud to be a part of the tribe.

It hasn't helped a lot to be a savage comic-book character for the last fifteen years—a drunken screwball who should've been castrated a long time ago. The smart people in the media knew it was a weird exaggeration. The dumb ones took it seriously and warned their children to stay way from me at all costs. The *really* smart ones understood it was only a censored, kind of toned-down children's-book version of the real thing.

Now we are being herded into the nineties, which looks like it is going to be a *true* generation of swine, a decade run by cops with no humor, with dead heroes, and diminished expectations, a decade that will go down in history as The Gray Area. At the end of the decade no one will be sure of anything except that you *must* obey the rules, sex will kill you, politicians lie, rain is poison, and the world is run by whores. These are terrible things to have to know in your life, even if you're rich.

Since that's become the mode, that sort of thinking has taken over the media as it has business and politics: "I'm going to turn you in, son—not only for your own good but because you were the bastard who turned *me* in last year."

This vilification by Nazi elements within the media has not only given me a fierce joy to continue my work—more and more alone out here, as darkness falls on the barricades—but has also made me profoundly orgasmic, mysteriously rich, and constantly at war with those vengeful retro-fascist elements of the Establishment that have hounded me all my life. It has also made me wise, shrewd and crazy on a level that can only be known by those who have been there.

WM: Some libraries classify *Fear and Loathing in Las Vegas* as a travelogue, some classify it as non-fiction, and some classify it as a novel. How much of this book is true? How would you characterize this book (beyond the jacket copy info in *The Great Shark Hunt*)? You refer to it as a failed experiment in Gonzo journalism, yet many critics consider it a masterwork. How would you rate it?

HST: *Fear and Loathing in Las Vegas* is a masterwork. However, true gonzo journalism as I conceive it shouldn't be rewritten.

I would classify it, in Truman Capote's words, as a non-fiction novel in that almost all of it was true or did happen. I warped a few things, but it was a pretty accurate picture. It was an incredible feat of balance more than literature. That's why I called it *Fear and Loathing*. It was a pretty pure experience that turned into a very pure piece of writing. It's as good as *The Great Gatsby* and better than *The Sun Also Rises*.

WM: For years your readers have heard about *The Rum Diary*. Are you working on it, or on any other novel? Do you have an ambition to write fiction? Your stint as a newspaper columnist was successful, but do you have further ambitions within journalism?

HST: I've always had and still do have an ambition to write fiction. I've never had any real ambition within journalism, but events and fate and my own sense of fun keep taking me back for money, political reasons, and because I'm a warrior. I haven't found a drug yet that can get you anywhere near as high as sitting at a desk writing, trying to imagine a story no matter how bizarre it is as much as going out and getting into the weirdness of reality and doing a little time on The Proud Highway.

The Rum Diary is currently under cannibalization and transmogrification into a very strange movie.

I am now working on my final statement—*Polo is My Life,* which is a finely muted saga of sex, treachery and violence in the 1990s, which also solves the murder of John F. Kennedy.

Notes and References

Chapter One

1. Daniel R. Baldwin, "Thompson Hunting: A Search for Hunter Thompson, a Quest for the American Dream" (M.A. thesis, University of Iowa, 1983), 27.

2. Pamela Lansden, "Take One," *People,* 25 November 1988, 53.

3. "Boy on First Job at Bank Finds 1st Pay Goes Too Far—Away," *Courier-Journal* [Louisville, Kentucky], 2 July 1953.

4. "Lost $50 Greets Owner Returning to Restaurant," *Courier-Journal,* 3 July 1953.

5. Kate Stout, "Hunter Thompson Used to Be a Kid?" *Louisville Today,* November 1980, 24.

6. Ibid., 25.

7. "3 High School Students Held for $8 Robbery in Park," *Courier-Journal,* 12 May 1955.

8. "3 High School Seniors Held in Robbery," *Louisville Times,* 11 May 1955.

9. "Tearful Youth Is Jailed Amid Barrage of Pleas," *Courier-Journal,* 16 June 1955.

10. "Youth Ordered Jailed for 60 Days Pending Action in Robbery Case," *Louisville Times,* 16 June 1955.

11. "Youth Is Fined in Scrape Halting His Graduation," *Courier-Journal,* 13 June 1955.

12. " 'Doing Better,' Youth Given His Freedom," *Louisville Times,* 18 August 1955.

13. Stout, "Thompson Used to Be a Kid?" 70.

14. Ibid., 25.

15. The comments in this and the following paragraph are drawn from W. S. Evans (Colonel, USAF), "Personnel Report: A/2C Hunter S. Thompson," 23 August 1957, reprinted in Hunter S. Thompson, *The Great Shark Hunt* (New York: Summit Books, 1979), v.

16. Baldwin, "Search for Hunter Thompson," 17.

17. These adventures are summarized in Craig Vetter, "Playboy Interview: Hunter Thompson," *Playboy,* November 1974, 75.

18. Ibid.

19. Peter O. Whitmer, "Hunter Thompson: Still Crazy After All These Years?" *Saturday Review,* January/February 1984, 20

20. Ibid., 20.

21. Vetter, "Playboy Interview," 78.

22. Ibid., 78.

23. Ibid., 78.

24. Whitmer, "Still Crazy," 20.

25. Vetter, "Playboy Interview," 82.

26. Ibid., 76.

27. Robert Sam Anson, *Gone Crazy and Back Again* (Garden City, N.Y.: Doubleday, 1981), 162.

28. Vetter, "Playboy Interview," 88.

29. Charles Moritz, ed., *Current Biography Yearbook 1981* (New York: H. W. Wilson, 1982), 417.

30. Moritz, *Current Biography,* 418.

31. Vetter, "Playboy Interview," 86.

32. Anson, *Gone Crazy,* 161.

33. Ibid., 165.

34. Vetter, "Playboy Interview," 88.

35. Moritz, *Current Biography,* 418.

36. Ibid., 418.

37. Crawford Woods, "The Best Book on the Dope Decade," *New York Times Book Review,* 23 July 1972, 17

38. Anson, *Gone Crazy,* 199.

39. *Fear and Loathing: On the Campaign Trail '72* (San Francisco: Straight Arrow Books, 1973), 413–14.

40. Stout, "Thompson Used to Be a Kid", 69.

41. Ibid., 70.

42. *Generation of Swine* (New York: Summit Books, 1988), 10.

43. Whitmer, "Still Crazy,"60.

44. Ibid., 60

Chapter Two

1. Edward E. Scharff, *Worldly Power* (New York: New American Library, 1986), 176.

2. *National Observer,* 6 August 1962, 13.

3. "A Footloose American in a Smuggler's Den," *National Observer,* 6 August 1962, 13.

4. "Renfro Valley," *Chicago Tribune,* 18 February 1962, and "Memoirs of a Wretched Weekend in Washington," *Boston Globe,* 23 February 1969.

5. *National Observer,* 27 August 1962, 16.

6. "Chatty Letters during a Journey from Aruba to Rio," *National Observer,* 31 December, 1967, 14.

7. Ibid., 14.

8. Ibid.

9. Ibid.

10. "Beer Boat Blues," *Courier-Journal and Times Magazine,* 11 November 1962.

11. Ernest Hemingway, "A Brush with Death," in *Byline: Ernest Hemingway,* ed. William White (New York: Scribner's, 1967), 275.

12. Ernest Hemingway, "A New Kind of War," in *Byline,* Ed. White, 262–63.

13. "Brazilian Soldiers Stage a Raid in Revenge," *National Observer,* 11 February 1963, 13.

14. "He Haunts the Ruins of His Once-Great Empire," *National Observer,* 10 June 1963, 13.

15. *National Observer,* 19 August 1963, 18.

16. "Why Anti-Gringo Winds Often Blow South of the Border," *National Observer,* 19 August 1963, 18.

17. William Plummer, "The Great Shark Hunt," *New Republic,* 25 August 1979, 37.

18. Tom Wolfe, (cf. p. 227) *The New Journalism* (New York: Harper & Row, 1973), 5.

19. Tom Wolfe, *The Kandy-Kolored Tangerine-Flake Streamline Baby* (New York: Farrar, Straus & Giroux, 1965), xii–xiii.

20. "What Lured Hemingway to Ketchum?" *National Observer,* 25 May 1964, 13.

21. "The Catch Is Limited in Indians' 'Fish-In,' " *National Observer,* 9 March 1964, 13.

22. "The Nonstudent Left," *Nation,* 27 September 1965, 154.

Chapter Three

1. "Motorcycle Gangs: Losers and Outsiders," *Nation,* 15 May 1965, 522.

2. Michael L. Johnson, *The New Journalism* (Lawrence: University Press of Kansas, 1971), 131.

3. "The Motorcycle Gangs: Hell's Angels," *Courier-Journal and Times Magazine,* 16 February 1967, 8.

4. "Losers and Outsiders," 523.

5. Ibid., 526.

6. Ibid., 9.

7. Moritz, *Current Biography,* 417.

8. Vetter, "Playboy Interview," 78.

9. "Motorcycle Gangs," 10.

10. Vetter, "Playboy Interview," 82.

11. *Hell's Angels* (New York: Ballantine, 1967), 11.

12. Johnson, *New Journalism,* 133.

13. Ibid., 131.

14. Tom Wolfe, *The Electric Kool-Aid Acid Test* (New York: Farrar, Straus & Giroux, 1968), 170.

15. Wolfe, *New Journalism,* 340.

16. *Hell's Angels,* 174.

17. Ibid., 175.

18. Ibid., 187.

19. Ibid., 51–52.

20. Ibid., 66.

21. P. J. O'Rourke, "Hunter S. Thompson," *Rolling Stone,* 5 November 1967, 232.

22. *Hell's Angels,* 348.

23. William James Smith, "Lessons in Anti-Social Behavior," *Commonweal,* 7 April 1967, 96.

24. Ibid., 97.

25. Wolfe, *Acid Test,* 170.

26. "Motorcycle Gangs," 13.

27. Leo E. Litwak, "On the Wild Side," *New York Times Book Review,* 7 April 1967, 6.

28. O'Rourke, "Hunter S. Thompson," 232.

29. Paul Thomas Meyers, "The New Journalist as Culture Critic" (Seattle: Washington State University, 1983), 159.

Chapter Four

1. J. Anthony Lukas, "The Prince of Gonzo," in *Stop the Presses, I Want to Get Off,* Ed. Richard Pollack (New York: Random House, 1975), 184.

2. Herbert Mitgang, "The Art of Insults Is Back, Gonzo Style," *New York Times,* 11 August 1988, 17N.

3. John Filiatreau, "Who Is Raoul Duke?" *Courier-Journal* 23 October 1975, E7.

4. James Green, "Gonzo," *Journal of Popular Culture,* (Summer 1975): 209.

5. "The Temptations of Jean-Claude Killy," in *The Great Shark Hunt* (New York: Summit Books, 1979), 77.

6. Ibid., 78.

7. Ibid.

8. Ibid., 83.

9. Ibid., 85.

10. Ibid.

11. Ibid., 86.

12. Ibid.

13. Ibid., 88.

14. Ibid., 94.

15. Ibid., 91.

16. Ibid., 90.

17. "The Kentucky Derby Is Decadent and Depraved," in *The Great Shark Hunt,* 25–26.

18. Ibid., 29–31.

19. Wolfe, *New Journalism,* 172.

20. "Kentucky Derby," 37–38.

21. Used in *Hell's Angels* and *Fear and Loathing in Las Vegas.*

22. "Kentucky Derby," 30.

23. John Hellmann, *Fables of Fact: The New Journalism as New Fiction* (Urbana: University of Illinois Press, 1981), 69.

24. Vetter, "Playboy Interview," 88.

25. Wolfe, *New Journalism* 15.

26. Plummer, "Great Shark Hunt," 37.

27. "Strange Rumblings in Aztlan," in *The Great Shark Hunt,* 136.

28. Ibid., 134.

29. Ibid., 142.

30. Gene Lyons, "How Stoned Were You?" *Nation,* 13 October 1979, 342.

Chapter Five

1. Robert Sam Anson, *Gone Crazy,* 159.

2. "Jacket Copy for Fear and Loathing in Las Vegas: A Savage Journey to the Heart of the American Dream," in *The Great Shark Hunt,* 106.

3. Jennifer Parmless, "The Caricature . . . the Writer . . . the Man," *Courier-Journal,* 10 January 1982, G13.

4. "Jacket Copy," 106.

5. Ibid., 108.

6. Wolfe, *Acid Test,* 169.

7. "Jacket Copy," 109.

8. *Fear and Loathing in Las Vegas* (New York: Warner, 1982), 3.

9. Ibid., 27.

10. Ibid., 39–40.

11. Ibid., 44.

12. Ibid., 46.

13. Ibid., 47–48.

14. Ibid., 108.

15. Ibid., 110.

16. Ibid.

17. Ibid., 114–15.

18. Ibid., 122–23.

19. Ibid., 130.

20. Ibid., 143.

21. Ibid.

22. Ibid., 156.

23. Ibid., 200.

24. Ibid., 203.

25. Ibid., 89.

26. Ibid., 68.

27. Crawford Woods, "Best Book," 17.

28. Hellmann, *Fables of Fact,* 75.

29. *Las Vegas,* 87.

30. Hellmann, *Fables of Fact,* 80.

31. Woods, "Best Book on the Dope Decade," 17.

32. *"Fear and Loathing in Las Vegas," New Republic,* 14 October 1972, 31–32.

33. "Jacket Copy," 109.

34. Ibid., 110.

Chapter Six

1. Anson, *Gone Crazy,* 176.

2. Timothy Crouse, *The Boys on the Bus* (New York: Random House, 1973).

3. Anson, *Gone Crazy,* 199.

4. Ibid.

5. Crouse tells the story of *New York Times* reporter R. W. Apple's experiences with a timid group of editors. Apple had correctly analyzed a McGovern tactic during the Democratic National Convention and transmitted a story containing this interpretation to New York. The story was not used, because no other newspaper or broadcast news organization offered the same analysis (*Boys on the Bus,* 87).

6. Ibid., ix.

7. *Campaign Trail,* 30–31.

8. Vetter, "Playboy Interview," 86.

9. Ibid.

10. *Campaign Trail,* 108.

11. Ibid., 109.

12. Ibid., 324.

13. Ibid., 413–14.

14. Ibid., 505.

15. "Catcher in the Wry," *Newsweek,* 1 May 1972, 65.

16. Steven D'Arazien, "Wild Man's View of the Campaign," *Nation,* 13 August 1973, 120.

17. Wayne C. Booth, "Loathing and Ignorance on the Campaign Trail: 1972," *Columbia Journalism Review* 19, no. 5 (November–December 1973): 7.

18. Ibid., 10.

19. Ibid., 11.

20. Ibid., 12.

21. Green, "Gonzo," 208.

22. "Fear and Loathing in Washington: The Boys in the Bag," in *The Great Shark Hunt,* 286.

23. Hunter S. Thompson, "Memo from the Sports Desk and Rude Notes from a Decompression Chamber in Miami," in *The Great Shark Hunt,* 241.

24. "Memo," 238.

25. Thompson tells the story of this encounter in "Presenting the Richard Nixon Doll (Overhauled 1968 Model)," *Pageant,* July 1968; reprinted in *The Great Shark Hunt,* 185–91.

26. "Memo," 239.

27. Ibid., 247.

28. "Fear and Loathing at the Watergate: Mr. Nixon Has Cashed His Check," in *The Great Shark Hunt,* 249.

29. "Watergate," 250.

30. Ibid., 282.

31. "Fear and Loathing in the Bunker," *New York Times,* 1 January 1974, 19.

32. "Fear and Loathing in Limbo: The Scum Also Rises," in *The Great Shark Hunt,* 302.

33. "Limbo," 318.

34. Ibid.

Chapter Seven

1. Vetter, "Playboy Interview,:" 88.

2. Ibid.

3. Ibid., 90.

4. "Richard Nixon Doll," 191.

5. *Rolling Stone,* 28 February 1974, 28.

6. "Fear and Loathing at the Super Bowl," in *The Great Shark Hunt,* 47.

7. Ibid.

8. Ibid., 48

9. Ibid., 53

10. Ibid., 57–58.

11. Ibid., 69.

12. Harold Conrad, "Fear and Loathing in Hunter Thompson," *Spin,* May 1986, 81.

13. Whitmer, "Still Crazy," 19.

14. "Super Bowl," 62.

15. Ibid., 66.

16. Ibid., 76.

17. Anson, *Gone Crazy,* 308.

18. George Plimpton, *Paper Lion* (New York: Putnam, 1966).

19. George Plimpton, *Shadow Box* (New York: Putnam, 1977).

20. Ibid., 257.

21. Ibid., 251.

22. "Last Tango in Vegas: Fear and Loathing in the Near Room," in *The Great Shark Hunt,* 547.

23. Ibid., 589.

24. Ibid., 587.

25. Ibid., 589.

26. Ibid.

27. Ibid., 587.

28. Ralph Steadman, *America* (San Francisco: Straight Arrow Books, 1974).

29. "Introduction," in Steadman, *America,* ii.

30. Stout, "Thompson Used to Be a Kid," 25.

31. *Playboy,* December 1974, 183.

32. "The Great Shark Hunt," in *The Great Shark Hunt,* 424.

33. Ibid., 433.

34. *Esquire,* April 1936, 61.

35. *Holiday,* July 1949, 60.

36. *Esquire,* October 1935; reprinted in *Byline,* ed. White, 213.

37. Ernest Hemingway, "Monologue to the Maestro: A High Seas Letter," in *Byline,* Ed. White, 214.

38. Ibid., 215.

39. "Shark Hunt," 436.

40. Ibid., 438.

41. Ibid., 452.

42. *The Curse of Lono* (New York: Bantam, 1983).

43. Whitmer, "Still Crazy," 60.

44. *Lono,* 28.

45. Richard Hough, *The Last Voyage of Captain Cook* (New York: Morrow, 1979).

46. *Lono,* 142.

47. Ibid., 150.

48. Ibid., 155.

49. Chris Haas, "The Curse of Lono," *New York Times Book Review,* 15 January 1984, 19.

Chapter Eight

1. Anson, *Gone Crazy,* 309.

2. Ibid., 311.

3. Ibid., 312.

4. *Rolling Stone,* 3 June 1976, 54.

5. "Jimmy Carter and the Great Leap of Faith," in *The Great Shark Hunt,* 458.

6. Ibid.

7. *Rolling Stone,* 3 June 1976.

8. *Rolling Stone,* 15 December 1977.

9. Interview with the author, 29 April 1978.

10. *The Great Shark Hunt,* 17.

11. Curtis Wilkie, "The Gonzo Historie," *Image,* 29 May 1988, 20.

12. H. L. Mencken, "Editorial," *American Mercury,* October 1925, 158–60.

13. Plummer, "Great Shark Hunt," 36.

14. William F. Buckley, Jr., "Gonzo's Great Shark Hunt," *New York Times Book Review,* 5 August 1979, 1.

15. Lyons, "How Stoned Were You" 342.

16. "A Dog Took My Place," *Rolling Stone,* 21 July–4 August 1983, 18.

17. Whitmer, "Still Crazy," 60.

18. "A Dog Took My Place," 25.

19. *Rolling Stone,* 9 May 1985, 47.

20. "Dance of the Doomed," 59.

21. Ibid.

22. Michael Herr, *Dispatches* (New York: Knopf, 1977).

23. "Strange Rumblings in Aztlan," 136.

24. Bill Beuttler, "A Finer Shade of Yellow," *American Way,* 1 June 1989, 123.

25. Ibid.

26. *Generation of Swine* (New York: Summit Books, 1988).

27. Ibid., 27.

28. Wilkie, "Gonzo Historie," 20.

29. *Generation of Swine,* 35.

29. Ibid., 9.

30. Ibid., 304.

31. Ibid., 10.

32. Mitgang, "Art of Insults," 17N.

33. Ibid.

34. Wilkie, "Gonzo Historie," 19–20.

35. Ibid., 20.

Chapter Nine

1. Conrad, "Fear and Loathing in Thompson," 52.

2. Stout, "Thompson Used to Be a Kid," 24.

3. Ibid., 25.

4. David Felton, "Gonzo Goes to Hollywood," *Rolling Stone,* 29 May 1980, 38.

5. Conrad, "Fear and Loathing in Thompson," 80.

6. Stout, "Thompson Used to Be a Kid," 70.

7. O'Rourke, "Hunter S. Thompson," 232.

8. Joseph Nocera, "How Hunter Thompson Killed the New Journalism," *Washington Monthly,* April 1981, 44.

9. Ibid., 46.

10. Ibid.

11. Robert J. VanDellen, "We've Been Had by the New Journalism," *Journal of Popular Culture* 10 (Summer 1975): 219.

12. Kent Jacobsen, "The Freaking New Journalism," *Journal of Popular Culture* 10 (Summer 1975) 185.

13. Wilkie, "Gonzo Historie," 19.

14. Plimpton, *Shadow Box,* 337.

Selected Bibliography

PRIMARY WORKS

Books

The Curse of Lono. New York: Bantam, 1983.
Fear and Loathing in Las Vegas. New York: Random House, 1972
Fear and Loathing: On the Campaign Trail '72. San Francisco: Straight Arrow
    Books, 1973.
Generation of Swine. New York: Summit Books, 1988.
The Great Shark Hunt. New York: Summit Books, 1979.
Hell's Angels. New York: Random House, 1967.
Songs of the Doomed. New York: Summit Books, 1990.

Articles

"Ask Not for Whom the Bell Tolls. . . ." *Rolling Stone,* 9 November 1972, 48.
"The Atmosphere Has Never Been Quite the Same." *National Observer,* 15 June
    1964, 1, 16.
"An Aussie Paul Bunyan Shows Our Loggers How." *National Observer,* 2 September
    1963, 2.
"Bagpipes Wail, Sabers Fly as the Clans Gather." *National Observer,* 4 September
    1964, 12.
"Ballots in Brazil Will Measure the Allure of Leftist Nationalism." *National Ob-
    server,* 1 October 1962, 4.
"The Banshee Screams for Buffalo Meat: Fear and Loathing in the Graveyard of the
    Weird." *Rolling Stone,* 15 December 1977, 48–59.
"The Battle of Aspen." *Rolling Stone,* 1 October 1970, 30–37.
"Beer Boat Blues." *Courier-Journal Magazine,* 11 November 1962.
"Brazilian's Fable of a Phony Carries the Touch of Mark Twain." *National Observer,*
    20 April 1964, 17.
"Brazilian Soldiers Stage a Raid in Revenge." *National Observer,* 11 February 1963,
    13.
"The Catch Is Limited in Indians' 'Fish-In.' " *National Observer,* 9 March 1964,
    13.
"Can Brazil Hold Out Until the Next Election?" *National Observer,* 28 October
    1963, 13.

"Chatty Letters during a Journey from Aruba to Rio." *National Observer*, 31 December 1962, 14.

"Collect Telegram from a Mad Dog." *Spider*, 13 October 1965.

"The Crow, a Novelist, and a Hunt: Man in Search of His Primitive Self." *National Observer*, 2 December 1963, 17.

"Dance of the Doomed." *Rolling Stone*, 9 May 1985, 47+.

"Democracy Dies in Peru, but Few Seem to Mourn Its Passing." *National Observer*, 27 August 1962, 16.

"Doctor Pflaum Looks at the Latins, but His View Is Tired and Foggy." *National Observer*, 9 March 1964, 19.

"A Dog Took My Place." *Rolling Stone*, 21 July–4 August 1983, 18–19.

"Donleavy Proves His Lunatic Humor Is Original." *National Observer*, 11 November 1963, 17.

"Election Watched as Barometer of Continent's Anti-Democratic Trend." *National Observer*, 20 May 1963, 12.

"Executives Crank Open Philosophy's Windows." *National Observer*, 9 September 1963, 13.

"Fear and Loathing: The Banshee Screams in Florida." *Rolling Stone*, 13 April 1972, 8–14.

"Fear and Loathing in the Bunker." *New York Times*. 1 January 1974, 19.

"Fear and Loathing in California: Traditional Politics with a Vengeance." *Rolling Stone*, 6 July 1972, 38–43.

"Fear and Loathing on the Campaign Trail '76: Third Rate Romance, Low Rent Rendezvous." *Rolling Stone*, 3 June 1976, 54.

"Fear and Loathing: Crank Time on the Low Road." *Rolling Stone*, 8 June 1972, 36–40.

"Fear and Loathing: In the Eye of the Hurricane." *Rolling Stone*, 20 July 1972, 22–24.

"Fear and Loathing: The Fat City Blues." *Rolling Stone*, 26 October 1972, 28–30.

"Fear and Loathing in Las Vegas, Part 1." *Rolling Stone*, 11 November 1971, 36–48 [Raoul Duke byline].

"Fear and Loathing in Las Vegas, Part 2." *Rolling Stone*, 25 November 1971, 38–50 [Raoul Duke byline].

"Fear and Loathing: Late News from the Bleak House." *Rolling Stone*, 11 May 1972, 26–32.

"Fear and Loathing in Limbo: The Scum Also Rises." *Rolling Stone*, 10 October 1974, 28–36, 49–52.

Fear and Loathing in Miami: Nixon Bites the Bomb." *Rolling Stone*, 28 September 1972, 30–46.

"Fear and Loathing in Miami: Old Bulls Meet the Butcher." *Rolling Stone*, 17 August 1972, 30–46.

"Fear and Loathing in New Hampshire." *Rolling Stone*, 2 March 1972, 6–12.

"Fear and Loathing in Saigon: Interdicted Dispatch from the Global Affairs Desk."
   Rolling Stone, 22 May 1975, 32–35.
"Fear and Loathing at the Super Bowl." *Rolling Stone,* 28 February 1974, 28–38,
   42–52.
"Fear and Loathing at the Super Bowl: No Rest for the Wretched." *Rolling Stone,*
   15 February 1973, 10.
"Fear and Loathing: The View from Key Biscayne." *Rolling Stone,* 16 March 1972,
   14.
"Fear and Loathing in Washington: The Million-Pound Shithammer." *Rolling
   Stone,* 3 February 1972, 6–10.
"Fear and Loathing in Washington: Is This Trip Necessary?" *Rolling Stone,* 6 Janu-
   ary 1972. 5–8.
"Fear and Loathing in Washington: It Was a Nice Place, They Were Principled
   People Generally." *Rolling Stone,* 4 July 1974, 42–47.
"Fear and Loathing at the Watergate: Mr. Nixon Has Cashed His Check." *Rolling
   Stone,* 27 September 1973, 30–39, 73–92.
"Fear and Loathing in Wisconsin." *Rolling Stone,* 27 April 1972, 12.
"A Footloose American in a Smugglers' Den." *National Observer,* 6 August 1962,
   13.
"Golding Tries 'Lord of the Flies' Formula Again, but It Falls Short." *National Ob-
   server,* 27 April 1964, 17.
"The Great Shark Hunt." *Playboy,* 1974 December 183+.
"The 'Hashbury' Is the Capital of the Hippies." *New York Times Magazine,* 14
   May 1967, 28–29+.
"He Haunts the Ruins of His Once-Great Empire." *National Observer,* 10 June
   1963, 13.
"How Democracy Is Nudged Ahead in Ecuador." *National Observer,* 17 September
   1962, 13.
"It's a Dictatorship, but Few Seem to Care Enough to Stay and Fight." *National
   Observer,* 28 January 1963, 17.
"Kelso Looks Just Like Any $1,307,000 Horse . . . A Day With a Champion."
   National Observer, 15 July 1963, 1.
"The Kentucky Derby Is Decadent and Depraved." *Scanlan's Monthly,* June 1970,
   1–12.
"Last Tango in Vegas: Fear and Loathing in the Far Room." *Rolling Stone,* 18 May
   1978, 62–68, 98–100.
"Last Tango in Vegas: Fear and Loathing in the Near Room." *Rolling Stone,* 4 May
   1978, 40–46.
" 'Leary Optimism' at Home for Kennedy Visitor." *National Observer,* 24 June
   1962, 11.
"Leftist Trend and Empty Treasury Plague the Latin American Giant." *National
   Observer,* 11 March 1963, 11.
"Life Styles: The Cyclist." *Esquire,* January 1967, 57–63.

"Living in the Time of Alger, Greeley, Debs." *National Observer*, 13 July 1964, 1, 16.

"Memoirs of a Wretched Weekend in Washington." *Boston Globe*, 23 February 1969, 6, 11.

"Memo from the Sports Desk and Rude Notes from a Decompression Chamber in Miami." *Rolling Stone*, 2 August 1973, 8–10 [Raoul Duke byline in part].

"Memo from the Sports Desk: The So-called 'Jesus Freak' Scare." *Rolling Stone*, 2 September 1971, 24 [Raoul Duke byline].

"Motorcycle Gangs: Hell's Angels." *Courier-Journal and Times Magazine*, 26 February 1967, 8.

"Motorcycle Gangs: Losers and Outsiders." *Nation*, 17 May 1965, 522–26.

"A Never-never Land High above the Sea." *National Observer*, 15 April 1963, 11.

"Nobody Is Neutral under Aruba's Hot Sun." *National Observer*, 16 July 1962, 14.

"Nonstudent Left." *Nation*, 27 September 1965, 154–58.

"And Now a Proletariat on Aspen's Ski Slopes." *National Observer*, 10 February 1964, 12.

"One of the Darkest Documents Ever Put Down Is 'The Red Lances.' " *National Observer*, 7 October 1963, 19.

"Operation Triangular: Bolivia's Fate Rides with It." *National Observer*, 15 October 1962, 13.

"People Want Bad Taste . . . in Everything." *National Observer*, 2 November 1964, 1, 15.

"Police Chief—The Indispensable Magazine of Law Enforcement." *Scanlan's Monthly*, September 1970, 63–66 [Raoul Duke byline].

"Presenting: The Richard Nixon Doll." *Pageant*, July 1968, 6–16.

"Renfro Valley." *Chicago Tribune*, 18 February 1962.

"Scar-strangled Banger." *Playboy*, May 1988, 95–97.

"The Sequins Were Michael's Idea." *Rolling Stone*, 30 August 1984, 52.

"Southern City with Northern Problems." *Reporter*, 19 December 1963, 26–29.

"Strange Rumblings in Aztlan." *Rolling Stone*, 29 April 1971, 30–37.

"A Surgeon's Fingers Fashion a Literary Career." *National Observer*, 21 December 1964, 17.

"The Temptations of Jean-Claude Killy." *Scanlan's Monthly*, March 1970, 89–100.

"Those Daring Young Men in Their Flying Machines." *Pageant*, September 1969, 68–78.

"A Time for Sittin', Listenin', and Reverie." *National Observer*, 3 June 1963, 16.

"Time Warp: Campaign '72." *Rolling Stone*, 5 July 1973, 48–62.

"Troubled Brazil Holds Key Vote." *National Observer*, 7 January 1963, 1.

"The Ultimate Freelancer." *The Distant Drummer*, November 1967.

"Uruguay Goes to Polls, with Economy Sagging." *National Observer*, 19 November 1962, 14.

"What Lured Hemingway to Ketchum?" *National Observer,* 25 May 1964, 1, 13.
"What Miners Lost in Taking an Irishman." *National Observer,* 16 December 1963, 4.
"When the Beatniks Were Social Lions." *National Observer,* 20 April 1964, 1, 14.
"When Buck Fever Hits Larkspur's Slopes." *National Observer,* 16 December 1963, 13.
"When the Thumb Was a Ticket to Adventures on the Highway . . . The Extinct Hitchhiker." *National Observer,* 22 July 1963, 12.
"Where Are the Writing Talents of Yesteryear?" *National Observer,* 5 August 1963, 17.
"Whither the Old Copper Capital of the West? To Boom or Bust?" *National Observer,* 1 June 1964, 13.
"Why Anti-Gringo Winds Often Blow South of the Border."*National Observer,* 19 August 1963, 18.
"Why Boys Will Be Girls." *Pageant,* August 1967, 94–101.
"Why Montana's 'Shanty Irishman' Corrals Votes Year after Year." *National Observer,* 22 June 1964, 22.
"You'd Be Fried Like a Piece of Lean Bacon." *National Observer,* 18 September 1964, 1, 19.

Miscellaneous

"From 'Fear and Loathing at the Super Bowl.' " In *Reporting: The Rolling Stone Style,* edited by Paul Scanlon, 215–29. Garden City, N.Y.: Doubleday, 1977.
"From 'Hell's Angels, a Strange and Terrible Saga.' " In *The New Journalism,* edited by Tom Wolfe, 340–55. New York: Harper & Row, 1973.
"Introduction." In *America,* by Ralph Steadman. San Francisco: Straight Arrow Press, 1974.
"The Kentucky Derby Is Decadent and Depraved." In *The New Journalism,* edited by Tom Wolfe, 172–87. New York: Harper & Row, 1973.

SECONDARY WORKS

Bibliography

Winship, Kihm. "Bibliography of Works by Dr. Hunter S. Thompson." In *The Great Shark Hunt,* 591–97. New York: Summit Books, 1979.
————. "Bibliography of Works on Dr. Hunter S. Thompson." In *The Great Shark Hunt,* 599–602. New York: Summit Books, 1979.

Monographs and Theses

Baldwin, Daniel R. "Thompson Hunting: A Search for Hunter Thompson, a Quest for the American Dream." M.A. thesis, University of Iowa, 1983.

Hellmann, Jerome. *Fables of Fact.* Urbana: University of Illinois Press, 1981.

Klinkowitz, Jerome. *The Life of Fiction.* Urbana: University of Illinois Press, 1977.

Meyers, Paul Thomas. "The New Journalist as Culture Critic: Wolfe, Thompson, Talese." M. A. thesis, Washington State University, 1983.

Wolfe, Tom. *The New Journalism.* New York: Harper & Row, 1973.

"Thompson, Hunter." In *Contemporary Authors,* vols. 19–20, 429–30. Detroit: Gale, 1968.

Articles about Thompson

Allen, Henry. "For Hunter Thompson, Outrage Is the Only Way Out." *Washington Post Book World,* 23 July 1972, 4.

Allis, Sam. "An Evening (Gasp!) with Hunter Thompson." *Time,* 22 January 1990, 64.

Anson, Robert Sam. "The *Rolling Stone* Saga, Part 2." *New Times,* 10 December 1976, 22+.

"Aspen Rejects Bid of Hippie Candidate for Sherriff's Office." *New York Times,* 5 November 1970, 32.

Booth, Wayne. "Loathing and Ignorance on the Campaign Trail: 1972." *Columbia Journalism Review* 19, no. 5 (November 1973):7–12.

Buckley, T. "Behind the Best Sellers." *New York Times Book Review,* 14 October 1979, 54.

"Catcher in the Wry." *Newsweek,* 1 May 1972, 65.

"Checking In with Dr. Gonzo." *Playboy,* November 1976, 254.

Conrad, Harold. "Fear and Loathing in Hunter Thompson." *Spin,* May 1986, 50–52, 79–81.

Crichton, J. "Fear and Loathing in Hawaii: Hunter Thompson Has New Bantam Book." *Publishers Weekly,* 1 July 1983, 69+.

Felton, David. "Gonzo Goes to Hollywood." *Rolling Stone,* 29 May 1980, 38–41.

Goffin, Gene. "Paranoia and Wild Turkey: Hunter Thompson in Buffalo." *Buffalo New Times,* 3 March 1974.

Green, James. "Gonzo." *Journal of Popular Culture* 9, no. 1 (Summer 1975):204–10.

Griffith, Thomas. "Fear and Loathing and Ripping Off." *Time,* 19 July 1976, 52–53.

Hinckle, Warren. "The Sworn Statement." *Image,* 29 May 1988, 13.

"Hunter Thompson: Commando Journalist." *Playboy,* November 1973, 188.

Jacobsen, Kent. "The Freaking New Journalism." *Journal of Popular Culture* 9, no. 1 (Summer 1975):183–86.

Jenkins, Loren. "Dr. Hunter S. Thompson and the Last Battle of Aspen." *Smart,* January–February 1990, 38–46.

Landreth, Elizabeth. "There Shall Be No Night." *Journal of Popular Culture* 19, no. 1 (Summer 1975):197–203.

Lukas, J. Anthony. "The Prince of Gonzo." *More: Journalism Review* (November 1972):4–7. Reprinted in Richard Pollock, ed. *Stop the Presses, I Want to Get Off.* New York: Random House, 1975.

Mandell, Arnold J., M.D. "Dr. Hunter S. Thompson and a New Psychiatry." *Psychiatry Digest* (37):12–17.

McCumber, David. "Fear and Trembling at the Examiner." *Image,* 29 May 1988, 14–18.

Nichols, Lewis. "In and Out of Books." *New York Times Book Review,* 5 March 1967, 8.

Nucera, J. "How Hunter Thompson Killed New Journalism." *Washington Monthly,* April 1981, 44–50.

O'Rourke, P. J. "Hunter S. Thompson." *Rolling Stone,* 5 November—10 December 1987, 230–32.

Plimpton, George. "The Last Laugh." *New York Review of Books,* 4 August 1977, 29.

Ripley, Anthony. " 'Freak Power' Candidate May Be the Next Sheriff in Placid Aspen, Colorado." *New York Times,* 19 October 1970, 44.

Roberts, Edwin A., Jr. "Will Aspen's Hippies Elect a Sheriff?" *National Observer,* 2 November 1970, 6.

Rosenbaum, Ron. "Hunter Thompson: The Good Doctor Tells All." *High Times,* September 1977, 31–39.

Rovner, Sandy. "Fear and Loathing at *Rolling Stone.*" *Washington Post,* 30 May 1975, B3.

Salisbury, Harrison. "Travels through America." *Esquire,* February 1976, 28+.

VanDellen, Robert J. "We've Been Had by the New Journalism." *Journal of Popular Culture* 9, no. 1 (Summer 1975):219.

Vetter, Craig. "Member of the Lynching." *Aspen Anthology* (Winter 1976):63–80.

————. "Playboy Interview: Hunter Thompson." *Playboy.* November 1974, 75+.

Vonnegut, Kurt, Jr. "A Political Disease." *Harper's,* July 1973, 92–94.

Whitmer, Peter. "Hunter Thompson: Still Crazy after All These Years?" *Saturday Review,* January/February 1984, 18–21+.

Wilkie, Curtis. "The Gonzo Historie." *Image,* 29 May 1988, 18–20.

Mentions of Thompson in Books

Acosta, Oscar Zeta. *The Autobiography of a Brown Buffalo.* San Francisco: Straight Arrow Books, 1972.

Anson, Robert Sam. *Gone Crazy and Back Again.* Garden City, N.Y.: Doubleday, 1981.

Crouse, Timothy. *The Boys on the Bus.* New York: Random House, 1973.

Mailer, Norman. *The Fight.* Boston: Little, Brown, 1975.

Perry, James M. *Us and Them: How the Press Covered the 1972 Election.* New York: Clarkson N. Potter, 1973.

Plimpton, George. *Shadow Box.* New York: Putnam, 1977.

Wolfe, Tom. *The Electric Kool-Aid Acid Test.* New York: Farrar, Straus & Giroux, 1968.

Index

The Author

William McKeen earned his bachelor's and master's degrees at Indiana University and his doctorate at the University of Oklahoma. A former newspaper reporter and editor in Indiana, Florida, Oklahoma, and Kentucky, he has taught at Western Kentucky University and the University of Oklahoma. He is associate professor of journalism and communications at the University of Florida. While working at the *Saturday Evening Post,* he was assistant editor of *The American Story,* an anthology published in 1975. He has contributed to *An Encyclopedia of American Humorists, The Biographical Dictionary of American Journalism,* and *Springboard to Journalism* and is the author of *The Beatles: A Bio-Bibliography* (1989). He has three children, Sarah, Graham, and Mary, and lives in Gainesville, Florida.

The Editor

Frank Day is a professor of English at Clemson University. He is the author of *Sir William Empson: An Annotated Bibliography* and *Arthur Koestler: A Guide to Research*. He was a Fulbright Lecturer in American Literature in Romania (1980–81) and in Bangladesh (1986–87).